Behind Every Smile

How to Spot and Support Victims of Trauma

By Natatia Vanellison

Published by NaTaTiaCoaching™ LLC
https://Behindeverysmilebook.com

For permissions, bulk orders, or speaking engagements, contact:
info@behindeverysmilebook.com

Printed in the United States of America
Manufactured by IngramSpark®

Library of Congress Control Number: 2025911396

U.S. Copyright Registration Number: TXu 2-498-100
Effective Date of Registration: June 10, 2025
Registration Decision Date: July 11, 2025

ISBN: 979-8-9932351-1-0
First Edition

Cover Design: Rose Reynolds, RoseReynolds & Co.
Back Cover Layout: Dana M. Mays, TaylorMade Creations™
(Creative Contributor, NaTaTiaCoaching™ LLC)
Author Photograph: Somi Benson-Jaja, Shot by Somi Studios

To my husband,
my rock, who never stopped believing in me.

To my mother-in-law,
who always showed me kindness and love.

And to my younger self,
this book is proof that you made it.

Contents

Introduction

I wish I could tell you that my story is one in a million.

But it's not.

The latest statistics show that one in four children grow up in some kind of abusive household in the United States.

That means 25 percent of the people you see each day are hiding trauma in their being. Having flashbacks daily. Believing they are not good enough now and never will be. Upholding a truth that love and relationships involve violence and pain. Isolating themselves from others because they lost the ability to connect. And like I did for decades, hiding behind a painted-on smile, so nobody has a clue.

But we can stop this from escalating exponentially.

We can learn how to pay attention to the signs people use to mask their pain. I will show you what symptoms to look for and possible ways to intervene.

I've been through the entire gamut of this cycle. I was a victim during my own childhood. And though I vowed not to, I unintentionally hurt other people when I got out of that situation.

But as the years passed, I became an educator, working with students who showed the same signs I used to hide. I went (and still go) to therapy to continue healing myself. And now, I am an advocate to help all survivors thrive.

I have made this my mission, and I now know why I endured those situations in the first place: to have empathy for those who are suffering and educate people how to help. This is no small feat, but I have this one life to do my best, and that is what I will do.

Since I have experienced multiple perspectives on this journey, my goal is to address each personality along the way. Whether you are currently a survivor, an abuser, a parent, an educator, a friend or someone who wants to help improve the mental stability of others in general (applause for you), you will walk away from this book with keen eyes and ears for sensing what somebody might be hiding, insights into how to approach and help them, and ways to heal yourself.

Look. I used to be that little girl who did everything I could *not* to go back home. I was told I would never amount to anything. I hid every personal aspect of my life because I feared the wrath.

But the way my formative years left me feeling was not who I was meant to be. I took the necessary steps to get help from therapy, educate myself and self-advocate to become the speaker and leader I am today.

If I can do it, anybody can.

The effect this book can have can be profound. It is my gift to the world to help you help others and yourself through the emotional baggage of the past. Doesn't a life with more joyful humans and less attachment to pain sound ideal?

If we continue to ignore the pain and trauma that hides below the surface of a quarter of the people in the USA, we will continue to see students going on shooting sprees at their school. We will continue to find a note as the last words a teenager left. And we will continue to let the hurting people inflict pain on their own children when they become parents, keeping the cycle going.

It is time to reclaim our humanity in a positive light with people who are ready to take charge of their lives and move forward with joy, respect and purpose. My hope is that this book will create a ripple effect for everyone who reads it.

Pass it on.

"You can't abuse me and tell me what to do with my pain."

— Darryl L. VanEllison

Part 1

Wounding

I bet you would be surprised at how many people around you are hiding behind their smile, stuffing their pain so deep that we can no longer see their wounds. However, we can still observe how that person reacts to the world from behind the lenses and the protective layers they wear.

How does a person get to this point?

They are wounded. So much of our perception of ourselves comes from how we were raised in our formative years. How we were treated. Whether we had access to love. All these pieces and more.

I have been that person hiding behind my smile. Writing this book has been a metaphorical stripping of the layers that I was hiding behind. Most of the people who know me will be shocked to read what's next, but it's time for me to bare my soul and share my story, so you understand you have permission to do the same with your wounds.

1

My Foundation

Growing up in the 1970s and 1980s, I witnessed domestic abuse almost daily.

But it wasn't what you might think.

My mother beat my father.

Though she was a foot shorter than him, she verbally, emotionally and physically abused my 6'4" tall, 200-pound teddy bear of a father.

My brother, sisters and I witnessed the cursing and beatings as a normal part of our lives.

Normal.

But we were not exempt from her wrath. Though my father got the brunt of the beatings, she saved plenty of emotional and verbal abuse to make sure we lived in fear and silence toward the outside world and herself.

Fast forward to June of 2015, when my father told us he had six months to live. For years, he had been secretly suffering from lung cancer. Only his *new* wife and her family knew.

My siblings and I went to visit him soon after we heard the news. I arrived at the home where he lived with his wife. Sitting on the bed, I saw a 6'4" skeleton with dark skin.

"Dad!" I shrieked under my breath.

I couldn't believe how frail he had become in such a short time, and we were just finding out.

But the other thing I noticed about him was *the glow*. You know, that glow around a person that signals their time here on earth is almost up. Not everyone can see that glow, but I can.

Sometimes I wish I couldn't.

I sat next to him on the bed and, knowing he wouldn't be in our lives much longer, I rubbed his back to comfort him.

And to comfort myself.

As I rubbed his back, I could feel the fragility of my father. His shoulder blades and backbone protruded more than ever. But as my hand swept the area between the bones—where the skin should have been smooth—I felt linear bumps running through his skin.

Those bumps were not from lung cancer. They were not from a deteriorating body.

They were from my mother's razor blade during a beating years before.

As my fingers touched the bumps, I shuddered, trying to deny where they came from. But when I looked at the open back of his hospital gown, I saw dozens of keloidal scars, antiquely clotted and raised. I had never seen them before, but my whole being flushed with anger as CPTSD kicked in, and my mind flashed back to the day my mother beat them into his frame.

That horrible day was a Sunday. For some reason, Sundays were my mother's worst day of the week. Probably because our father always took a ride somewhere else. My mother would get so fired up on Sundays, I would shout to my siblings, "Ooh, she's the devil!"

On that Sunday, my father went to his mother's house, my grandma's, in what I thought might be an attempt to leave for good.

My mother and my grandmother did not like each other. They were caught in a power struggle over my father. I don't know how my mother knew my father was up to something, but she suddenly became enraged and loaded us in her car.

Then she drove to my grandmother's house.

Real fast.

My mother always drove so fast that I still carry trauma and struggle to feel safe riding in a car when other people are driving. She drove so fast her eyeballs stared through the windshield like bullets as the car tried to keep up.

I realize now that I had a panic attack in the car that day. I think my siblings did too. We were crying and fearing for our lives to say the least.

As the Georgia Magnolias turned to cotton trees, and the gravel clouded up beneath our mother's tires as she flew around the corners, I knew we were almost to our grandmother's house.

She pulled up and got out, yelling, "Do *not* get out of this car! *Stay in this car!*" As she marched to the door, I looked at her hands. She did not have her knife on her, thank goodness. But I noticed she kept her fingers straight on her right hand. Just the way she taught us when hiding one of those old shaving razor blades between our middle and ring finger.

Though we dared not exit the car, we listened intently through the car windows that were still rolled down. My mother pounded on the door. We could not hear everything she said, but we heard our grandmother shout back, "You are as old as me, and too old for him anyway!"

This comment ignited my mother's fury, and she cussed at my grandmother some more. Then she shouted at my dad, "I know you're in there! Get your a** out the door!"

I still do not know why he came out. Probably so she would not take it out on us kids. He really was our protector.

I watched as he assessed her posture. He could tell by the angle of her hand that she was hiding one of her favorite secret weapons. She slapped his back and hit him repeatedly, cursing at him for every reason she could think of. We watched in horror from the car.

Once our mother tired out, our father removed his t-shirt, pulling up on the fresh wounds and sticky skin as it came over his head. Blood ran down his back, and the incision marks were instantly pink and puffy.

My siblings and I were still in the car crying hysterically and feeling utterly helpless. But I did not accept that feeling, so I screamed at my mother, "I hate you!"

Decades later, when I rubbed dad's old back, feeling the scars that remained, I relived that moment in my mind. I remembered time after time when she beat him in a similar way. Those bumps on his back signified a life lived not in fear, but perseverance. Because he didn't die by her hand after all.

And although part of me still wanted to hate her for all the terrible things she had done as I sat next to my pillar of a father, I couldn't.

I knew better.

I could only feel sorry for her.

See, my mother was not mentally stable. I could even tell back then. I always questioned her motives which made her want to break my spirit even more. "You think you're more than you are," she would hiss.

But I kept on. I knew she had no authority over me, and I could not wait to leave her house.

Like so many struggling people in the world, she needed help. She was hurting before she got married. Before she had kids. But instead of addressing her pain to help her become a more peaceful and stable person, she took it out on her family.

Had it been accessible or acceptable for her to get some counseling, things could have been different for all of us. But our little Georgia town was not set up to help people with their mental problems, and the stigma was "Don't tell anybody your business."

We too were forced to keep quiet. So early on, I learned to live two lives. One in the volatile environment of our home and one behind a smile at school.

I know now that I'm not the only one who has ever had to do this.

No matter where we live in this world, we likely encounter struggles. It's part of life and, ultimately, growth. But when people do not see that they have a choice in how to get through their struggles, they tend to blame others or themselves. Untreated anguish festers and can soon be projected onto others as verbal and emotional abuse or violence.

Just like I witnessed with my mother.

I designed this book to help people experiencing a similar situation. Whether you are the abuser (though you may not realize it yet), the survivor, the innocent bystander or the educator like I am now, I want to make sure you can recognize the signs that something isn't right. I want to empower you to be able to see when this is happening to someone else or yourself and find the strength to ask for help.

Because this should *never* keep happening. When you feel something is not right, say something. *Do* something. Reach out for help, no matter what your role is.

I have been in therapy for eleven years and counting. I did it to save my sanity. To save myself from the triggers of my past. And do you know what?

It's helping.

I am now able to lead a more normal life. But even more than that, a purposeful one. I speak out on behalf of others. I advocate. I educate educators on how to recognize this in the students and parents in their classes. I will no longer silence this voice like I was told to do so many times before.

That is not the solution.

The solution is recognizing when a situation does not feel right and doing something about it.

I was always smiling at school. In my double life, I never talked about my home when I finally had a chance to escape from it. Maybe somebody could have asked me what was going on behind my smile.

Please, be the person who asks.

2

Big Emotions

In order to analyze the hidden signs of people who are experiencing domestic violence, emotional abuse and verbal abuse, we must first understand the emotions they are still carrying and *trying* to hide.

Since I spent much of my life as a witness *and* a victim, I am most comfortable telling you about the main emotions I felt. We will get into other perspectives later.

Growing up in a household where I witnessed my mother torment my father first and foremost, and my siblings and I second, these are the debilitating emotions I was secretly dealing with in my home life and my "double life":

- Shame and guilt
- Unworthiness and low self-esteem
- Numbness
- Silence and Fear

These emotions ran so deep in me that I thought they were what I was made of. Despite that feeling, I did not want anyone to know they were part of me at all.

They did not feel right to me.

Let me just stop right here and really emphasize that if something *does not feel right* to you, it probably is not right. Trust your instincts on this. It's a very basic notion. And when you notice something is not right, I encourage you to find someone you trust to talk to about that notion, no matter what role you have in the situation.

But back to my "other life." My school life. My trying-to-escape-what-was-happening-at-home life. Please be aware that the signs of someone enduring abuse and violence in their life are often hidden.

I hid them myself.

And because I experienced them all so deeply, I know what to look for. As an educator, I've been called the "child whisperer." When a student would act out, I was often called upon to intervene. Because I knew what signs to look for and what questions to ask, I was able to make an impact.

Out of fear of judgement, I never came out and told my colleagues why or how I knew what I was doing, but I can see it's time to make a difference now. It's time for me to speak out and try to help our budding generations by educating and empowering the adults who teach, nurture and guide them.

If you have never been in an abusive situation before, consider yourself lucky. But in order to make the most difference, you will need to know what to look for.

Here are some insights on how to observe and decipher a person's actions and reactions in public when they are hiding deep emotions from another part of their life.

Shame and Guilt

Shame and guilt were big feelings that often caused me to hide inside myself. I grew up in a small town in Georgia, but I can imagine that any kid living anywhere would simply want to feel like they had a normal family with a normal life. But our house often had the police visit, and I was usually the one who called them.

I remember one time, when I was a teenager, things got so heated at home that my mother stabbed my father in the buttocks with an icepick. Boy, I tell you, I never knew what would set off the rage at home; but Dad was bleeding from his right cheek, so I had to call the police.

Again.

In those moments when the police arrived, I had to juggle being responsible for the call, standing up for my father, keeping my brothers and sisters calm, recounting what I witnessed if asked and—now this is the most shameful part for a teenager—looking out the window to see which neighbors noticed this time. Who would know? Who would say something at school?

I always prayed nobody would.

School was where I could go to pretend that this was not my life. That I was somebody else. I certainly did not want the shame and guilt to follow me there.

So I would be quiet. I was *really* quiet at school. I was smart and positive, and some teachers knew I was gifted. But I did my best not to speak if I did not have to, so nobody would know what I buried deep inside. Now, I'm already an introvert, but I had to go further within myself to be able to rebuild my energy. It was the safest place I could go.

I would often distract myself with fantasies that I created or read in books. Books (and later, soap operas) were my saving grace. They also led me to a place where things were not only "normal," but they could be beautiful and magical. I wanted to stay there as long as I could. Being in those other places helped me to strengthen my smile as a shield.

PsychologyToday.com has articles about this dissociative reaction in further detail. People need to go where they feel safe, so they do not crumble.

Some signs to look out for in someone who is experiencing shame and guilt can be:

- Remaining quiet unless spoken to
- Hiding in distractions of any kind
- Always smiling, even when it's not appropriate

When you encounter someone who exhibits these signs, simply ask them what is going on. They may not respond, which is another red flag, but keep observing them and look out for some of the following signs as well.

Unworthiness and Low Self-Esteem

I know that feelings of unworthiness and low self-esteem are normal emotions a person can harbor if they are in an abusive situation. If someone is constantly berating you, blaming you and telling you horrible things about yourself (that are not even true), you might start to believe them.

Once you believe them, your body changes. Your shoulders drop. You cower. You try to stay small, so you are not in anybody's way.

Though I know this, I still looked it up. I am always learning, and I love psychology, so here is another thing I learned at PsychologyToday.com: If you feel unworthy, you think you lack in excellence and believe you are not worthy of attention. You retract in life and become quiet.

Now I'll be honest that after I really dug into this in my years of research, I realized I did not necessarily react in that way. My siblings did that more than I did. *My* immediate reaction was to prove my mother wrong. I instantly became a rebel and an overachiever. To this day, I am always researching, always mentoring, always taking the next course that will prove I am smart and worthy of success.

Why?

Because I was told the opposite every day of my life. "You think you're more than you are," my mother would say. And when I told her I wanted to be a teacher, she scoffed, "All you're going to be doing is babysitting." I can see now that, in actuality, she was jealous of me because she wanted to be more than she was, but she was not. And to keep me her equal or below her, she devised a meager life for me—but I held fast to my aspirations.

I feel very fortunate that I was able to keep my positive outlook and perseverance through all that verbal and emotional abuse. And my therapist has shown me that my overachieving habits stem from being told I would never be good enough; although it is a part of me that I've grown to like, so I'll keep that.

Recognizing unworthiness and low self-esteem in someone can be challenging, but common signs include:

• Withdrawing or physically shrinking. This might look like slouching, avoiding eye contact or trying to make themselves "invisible" in social settings. According to the *National Institute of Mental Health (NIMH)*, these nonverbal cues often signal underlying feelings of inadequacy.

• Overachieving to prove worthiness. People constantly push themselves beyond limits. Not for personal growth, but out of fear of not being "enough." Dr. Kristin Neff, a leading researcher on self-compassion, highlights how this perfectionist mindset can mask self-worth struggles.

• Attention seeking. Engaging in behaviors that attract notice, even if it's negative, to feel validated. The *American Psychological Association (APA)* notes that this can stem from a deep-rooted need for external affirmation. When noticing these signs in someone you care about, consider the following approaches to offer support:

• Create a safe space. Encourage open conversations without judgment. Let them know they are seen and heard.

- Practice compassion. Remind them that self-worth isn't tied to achievements or external validation.
- Encourage professional support. Consult a coach, counselor, or therapist who can provide tailored strategies.
- Highlight strengths. Gently remind them of their unique qualities and past successes to reinforce positive self-perception.

Numbness

One element of my mother's violent habits that really affected my mood was whether or not blood was involved in the latest scene with my father. No blood meant I was still horrified at the latest event, and I would retract and be quiet. But blood often caused me to go numb.

Who wants to feel anything when tragedies like that *cause* the feelings? With all the tragedies I witnessed, I could easily have walked around as a blubbering mess. That would have made it obvious to my teachers.

But crying at home just got me into more trouble. I was told I was weak or whiny, so I numbed those feelings. They turned me a bit cold.

One way I adapted to living like this was laughing instead of crying. When something sad happened at school, I would laugh it off. I would not get in nearly as much trouble for laughing at home as if I cried.

But is laughing at a sad situation a normal reaction?

No. It's not.

In fact, some of my reactions to my hidden emotions caused other kids to think I was weird. I don't blame them. I probably did seem weird to them—always smiling and laughing at strange times. But that also caused them to bully me. Not so much where they would beat me up in the halls, but they would tease me.

One boy on the bus would try to hurt me by shouting, "Look at your gapped teeth! You are so black!"

As if I didn't know that. The irony was my brother and sister were not. Though we were born of the same parents, my siblings had fair skin and red hair. So as hard as it was for that bully (and most everyone else who knew our family) to figure out how that was possible, it completely baffled me.

This genetic expression was one of the reasons I thought I was adopted.

I was tough enough to handle bullying though. I would just hit them or cuss at them. That was my reaction. Even in first grade! I can remember my first-grade teacher saying, "Natatia, go to the sink and brush your teeth!" after each of my many episodes of profanity. But instead of toothpaste, I had to put Dial soap in my mouth. Some tastes you never forget.

Now, when it comes to bullying, I think teachers and administrators are pretty keen at seeing the bullies themselves as someone who needs attention. People hurt others because they are hurting, so they talk to the bully and ask what's going so wrong in their life that they need to pick on others.

Bullying is never okay, so this is a great strategy.

But don't forget to *observe the victim* of the bullying as well. What makes them an easy target? Are they weird? Are they quiet? Do they laugh at inappropriate times? Do they hit or use violence in reaction? Do they use profanity consistently and appropriately?

These types of words are almost always picked up from the environment. Research by Jay and Jay (2013) shows that kids can start using taboo words as early as twelve to twenty-four months, usually by mimicking what they hear from adults, peers or media. It is not something they naturally come up with; it is learned from the world around them.

Talking to the victim of bullying to see how they are doing after being affected by the bully is a great time for guidance counselors and other faculty to dig a little deeper to see if the little victim might be making themselves an easy target.

When you or someone you know reacts oddly in situations, please ask why. This reaction could be from an intentional detour in their brain. And if they react ferociously to bullying or other offenses, their reactions might be well-practiced… at home.

Silence and Fear

My siblings and I were told repeatedly, by both my mother and father, not to talk about what was happening in our home. It was nobody's business but ours, and it certainly was not something we wanted to publicize.

So I learned how to keep that silence out of fear – especially when my father requested it. He would say, "Don't tell people what happens in this house." I did my best to honor his wishes. But in doing so, I did not tell my teachers or friends, even when asked.

For instance, when I was in fourth grade, I was sent to see this blonde-haired, blue-eyed counselor. He asked me some good questions that possibly could have helped me figure out what was going on in my life.

But do you know what I did?

I lied.

I knew I *had* to lie because telling the truth would mean my siblings and I would be taken away from our parents. That is exactly what our father was trying to avoid.

Plus, the consequences of me telling an authority figure outside of those police calls would certainly come with punishment on its own. From my mother.

My siblings and I kept quiet to avoid this punishment. In fact, I got so good at keeping secrets that I started keeping all kinds of them—especially from my mother. I can see now that she was afraid of my potential and my spirit. Not only afraid, but jealous, and jealousy is often expressed in anger.

According to *Psychology Today*, some parents may experience envy toward their children, especially when the child possesses qualities or opportunities the parent lacked (Making the Whole Beautiful, 2022). My mother seemed to fear my potential and spirit, viewing them as a threat rather than a source of pride.

That fear often turns into jealousy, and as *Verywell Mind* explains, jealousy can quickly give rise to anger when feelings of inadequacy or resentment surface (Cherry, 2021). It is a complex dynamic, one that *Wikipedia's Narcissistic Parent* entry further clarifies: parents with unmet needs or unfulfilled ambitions may perceive their child's growth as a challenge to their self-worth. This perception can trigger controlling behaviors or emotional distance. Understanding this now does not erase the impact but helps me make peace with the silence I once lived in.

Like I brought up earlier, I wondered if I was adopted for much of my childhood. Not only did my siblings not share my skin and hair color, but they were allowed to have more of a life than I was. I was always told "no" when I wanted to do the same things they were doing. The same exact things! I could not figure out the double standard, so I figured I must have not been her real daughter.

My mother loved to control what I could and could not be a part of because she could not control my rebellious spirit. Whether my rebellion was the biggest reason she kept me on a leash, I cannot be sure. But it certainly did not seem fair, and it made me resent her more.

I would always speak up against her. Question her. Make her uneasy. My siblings never did that, so she felt safer allowing them to be individuals out in the world.

One example of this was the school band. My brother and sister were each allowed to try out for the band; she even paid for their lessons! But I was not even allowed to try out. So you know what I did? I tried out without telling her.

If I was going to play the clarinet in the band, I would figure it out on my own. I wanted to break her chains and have a life too. Besides, the more I had to keep me out of that house, the better.

I even tried out for the flag line in secret which required more coordination than I was trained for because we didn't dance at home. It was not allowed. I did not make the cut, but I was proud that I tried.

I had a boyfriend for a while in high school too. Did my mother know? No way. Everything I did outside of our home was kept private from my mother. Unless I was actively challenging her, I would tiptoe around her and live in deceit every waking moment of my existence in her presence.

On the flipside, everything that happened at home was kept private from my other life.

Can you see how this would severely alter the reality of a child? An adult even? Do you understand why it is so hard to be able to discern when your friends, students, neighbors, etc. are experiencing such turmoil? They are hiding it! It is buried so deep that they cannot even admit this dualism to themselves when they are in the "other" situation.

But we can look for evidence of secrets.

I've learned that we can find out a lot more from what people are not saying than what they are saying. Because, like me, they can lie to your face to make you stop asking questions. To make you think everything is fine.

Recognizing someone who is holding back may sound obvious, but unless you are trained, it's not. Luckily, experts define certain behaviors that offer clues. Here are a few signs to watch for in someone who is keeping deep secrets, along with ways to approach the situation:

- Fidgeting or avoiding eye contact. If someone can't sit still or struggles to make eye contact while sharing their story, it might signal discomfort or withholding of information (*Feldman, 2018*). A proper response to this sounds more like an invitation to a calm space instead of pressing for answers. You can say something like, "I'm here if you ever feel like talking more about it."
- Shifting or squirming when questioned. Squirming or frequent position changes can suggest anxiety or uncertainty about what to say (*Meetings & Conventions, 2020*). When you encounter this situation, it's important to acknowledge the person's feelings. You can say, "This might be hard to discuss. Take your time." Validating their difficult emotions and offering a time and space when they are ready can help diffuse their anxiety and plant the seed for a future conversation.
- Getting defensive or angry when pressed for details. A defensive reaction often masks vulnerability, especially when someone feels cornered (*HackSpirit, 2023*). Here, you want to avoid escalating the situation. Try saying, "It's okay if you don't want to talk about it right now." But let them know the offer stands.
- Portraying a "too perfect" life. Sometimes, people overcompensate by painting an ideal picture to hide their struggles (*HackSpirit, 2023*). You can gently open the door for honesty: "You always seem so put-together. When things ever feel different, I'm here."

Offering yourself as a trusted friend when someone is displaying these defensive behaviors, and giving them time to process, is a good start to opening up a place they can feel safe to talk. Pressure from you or anyone who wants to support them can cause a trigger and escalate their behavior to close them off more.

Be aware that what lies behind the lies is also what lies behind the smile.

3

Baggage

I would bet most of us have heard talk about how childhood trauma might affect us later in our lives. How it builds the foundation of who we think we are, who we think we should be and how we view the world.

The unfortunate thing is that any trauma or learned behavior does not disappear once we have grown into an adult. The memories are not forgotten once we move out of the house. The feelings we have about ourselves do not automatically change when we go out into the world on our own. In fact, it's quite the opposite.

When we pack our bags to move on in life, we are also carrying the weight of the heaviest bags of all: our emotional baggage.

The way people are affected by an upbringing full of verbal and emotional abuse will vary from person to person, that is a given. But as I share mine, I'm sure you can find some similar streams to relate to and, if you are the nurturer, to look out for.

The heaviest bags I carried contained:

- Negativity and powerlessness
- Inability to trust others

Those words are heavy in themselves. As I look back at those bags, I can see how burdensome even one of them would be to me today. But both of them? Whoo! It's a surprise I was able to walk at all!

But the irony is, I had no idea I was carrying them. Most of us do not realize when we are lugging all this around because it is consuming us. We are all wrapped up in it and are unaware of how it physically and mentally crushes us. It sort of *becomes* us, and we must first realize that fact before we can separate ourselves from that baggage and let it go.

That is where the work comes in.

Let's unzip those bags and try on what's inside to see how those afflictions used to fit.

Negativity and Powerlessness

Even looking at these words brings upon a darkness. An oppression. Overwhelm.

Because that is how I felt when I was living through them.

At age nineteen, I finally left the house I grew up in. When I walked out that door, part of me felt excited and free to do whatever I chose. The truth of it, however, was that I greatly lacked experience with the outside world, was quite numb, and felt scrambled in my brain.

Plus, I had very little money and no job. But my main priority was getting out of that house, so that is what I did. I found an apartment with some acquaintances and got a job at the JCPenney in Atlanta.

My mother's plan for me was to go to a local technical college, and she financially supported me in that endeavor when I left. Because it was her idea.

That was not *my* plan for me, but since I received compensation for it, it seemed like the safest bet at the time. I succeeded with a major in secretarial science, but I could feel that my heart was not going to blossom taking calls and filing papers for somebody else.

I wanted to teach.

"You'll only be babysitting other people's children," my mother would tell me each time I said this within her earshot. Of course, she wanted to take my power away by making my dream sound trivial and meaningless. But the way my heart swelled when I imagined myself in front of a class proved her wrong.

Not long after I moved out and attended that technical school, my roommates and I were unable to pay rent to keep our apartment, so I had to do the unthinkable.

Go back home.

This was 100 percent unfair to me because I was smart. *Really* smart, and I knew it. I loved to study, and I got the best grades. I would not let a technical degree in a field I did not care for while living with my horrible mother be the last for me. I knew I was destined for more, so I worked out a deal with my father. I promised him that I would get my degree in college and make him proud. He would never regret helping me, I just knew it.

But by the time I started applying for college, I was already on the path to enter as a non-traditional student. If that wasn't already slightly embarrassing as a young person, walking in to take the college entrance exam in my old high school with the kids in my younger brother's class turned it into torture. But I decided to be brave and face that challenge.

Those kids knew who I was, and they probably wondered what I was doing there after I graduated. But instead of letting their stares get to me, I kept my chin up, answered all the questions on the exam and got myself out of that room.

I did it.

And I did it totally against my mother's will. The grand irony was that my brother and sister were able to attend college *with* her blessing… and financial support. But when it came to me, she gave the excuse, "We don't have that kind of money to send you to college."

Again, was I adopted?

Or was she still trying to break me after I left?

No matter the answer, I knew better than to let her crush me. I would show her I could do anything I wanted, and I did not need her help.

That's how I ended up getting out of that house for good. For the next school year, I attended college and stayed in a dormitory thanks to my father. I am so grateful he truly believed in me and supported my dreams and goals. And, spoiler alert, I never let him down.

He was my saving grace. I don't know what I would have done without him because my mother was just the opposite. She wanted to keep me close. Keep me down. Keep me as low as she felt about herself.

When she found out I was going to college after all, she tried another power-stealing technique. She told me, "You're too old to go to school anyway." Luckily, I knew the words she said to me were uttered only to try to strip me of my strength. She tried every time, but that fueled me more to prove her wrong.

"Watch me," I glared. And eventually, I did prove her wrong.

When someone grows up with a parent who is always negative toward them (and everything else in the world), I feel they have two choices: crumble and succumb to the projected unworthiness *or* rebel and prove that parent wrong. Choosing the latter threw me into another category of over achievement, but it helped keep me motivated.

I wasn't necessarily motivated by success, however. I was motivated because I was afraid of failure. See, my mother, who was nowhere near perfect herself, somehow drilled it into me that I had to be perfect, or I would fail.

Besides her own negativity, I can now see that this notion was the root cause of my own negativity and fear of failure.

Pay attention now because these are the things I told myself. Be aware if you or anyone you know has this dialogue with themselves.

- I'm not good enough.
- I can't live up to the expectations of others.
- I'll never be perfect, and that is the only way to be worthy.

Being so afraid of failure also caused me to procrastinate on pretty much everything. Why would I want to start or finish something that was destined to fail? Procrastination allowed me to put off that feeling of failure as long as I possibly could. It was freedom for a little while longer. Then, of course, it became stressful at the last minute.

Years later, I stumbled upon a piece of writing that gave me exactly the quote I needed to create a new mantra. Though the author was listed as anonymous, the words shook me to my core: *"Perfection is fear, and excellence is the opposite of fear."* This powerful reminder came from the poem *Excellence vs. Perfection*, often shared through educational resources like the National Association of Schools of Art and Design (NASAD).

What a jolt to realize I had been living in fear all that time! It was so debilitating that I sometimes would not even do my work. But that quote made me realize I don't need perfection in my life. I don't even *want* it.

It is based in fear.

So I decided to change my negative self-talk and strive for excellence. It was difficult at first, and to this day, I still remind myself to focus on excellence instead of perfection. But luckily, it has been working like a dream.

The book *Daring Greatly* by Dr. Brené Brown also helped me shift my mindset. This book, and much of her work, showed me that these negative beliefs are simply perceptions. It showed me that trauma, mental illness and negative life experiences are what generate these power-stealing beliefs, so it becomes mandatory to stop those cycles of powerlessness.

As healing humans, we need to observe the way we talk to ourselves. We tend to believe what other people tell us, even if it hurts or isn't true. But the ongoing damage occurs when we start to believe these criticisms are true and go on to tell ourselves the same things we heard—or maybe even an exaggerated version of the insult. This perpetuates that cycle, and soon we begin to live our life in a way where we show up in this negative light because that's the part of us we focus on.

My mother was a shining example of this—a "negaholic," as Dr. Chérie Carter-Scott describes it. The term negaholic was originally coined by Dr. Chérie Carter-Scott in her book *Negaholics: How to Overcome Negativity and Turn Your Life Around.* This book explores habitual negativity and how to break free from limiting beliefs. A negaholic is addicted to negativity, unable to see possibilities beyond their own limiting beliefs (Carter-Scott, 1989). Their outlook is shaped by constant pessimism, an attachment to self-doubt, and a tendency to bring others into their cycle of negativity.

Growing up, I witnessed how this mindset shaped interactions, created barriers to joy, and reinforced a belief that life was meant to be endured rather than embraced.

In direct contrast, allow me to tell you a story about the first person I met whose light was a breath of fresh air. A refreshing feeling still comes over me as I remember her chewing peppermint gum and smelling fresh like Listerine. Surprisingly, she was not someone with a fancy job, but the person who cleaned up after them—and everybody else.

She was the custodian in my school.

She was so cheerful and complimentary that she would say something nice about whatever she could think of, including my outfit sometimes. And I could tell she was genuine.

After daily encounters with this cheerful custodian, I began to see that people could be different than I had learned in my house. Different than I had seen most everybody else be. And I wanted to be like her.

One day I told her, "When I grow up, I want to be a custodian just like you." I hope I made her day because she always made mine. And that is the essence of her that I choose to take with me.

When I interact with people in a room, I don't need to be perfect. I don't need to be the best. But when I leave, I hope I leave a little sparkle behind for people to see and feel. I want my shine to rub off on at least one person, so I can help make the world a brighter place.

Just like that custodian.

Inability to Trust Others

When I grew up repeatedly hearing the phrase, "Don't trust people outside this house," I evolved to be leery of people I didn't know. Besides that, my mother would say, "Men only want one thing from you," so I matured to believe that as well.

These phrases became a critical part of how I viewed the outside world. I can still hear them echo through my brain in her voice.

One might say that she was telling my siblings and me these things to protect us from the outside world. To make sure we had our shields up to ward off the evils of other human beings. But she was not preparing us for a battle *out there*. She was trying to keep us *in here*. She wanted us with her, so she wouldn't feel lonely, and she could keep control of us.

As menacing as that might sound, it's the truth. It was another way she emotionally abused us. She tried to make us fear the world outside, so we felt safe in our home with her as our dictator. This is also how cult leaders treat their followers. It's a control tactic.

So pay attention to what other parents say to their kids. Listen to what your students say back to you or their friends. Ask yourself what you might be telling your own children or yourself.

Phrases like, "The world outside is not safe," and "Don't trust people outside this house," have much different intention than questions that make children think for themselves like, "How was your day? What did you experience? How do you feel around other people? Other adults?" These phrases open a conversation and let the child think for themselves, which is exactly the opposite of what my mother wanted us, especially me, to do.

Even the classic, "Don't talk to strangers," advice gives a little more leeway than expecting the child not to trust anyone. The child needs to know there are people (i.e. teachers, neighbors, community members, etc.) that they can run to if they have trouble or need an adult.

The years I spent listening to her held me captive in my own instincts. I was not street smart. My common sense was tied up with most of my other life tools, and this probably showed on my face or in my body language when I was out in the world. And let me tell you, the world is ready to test young adults who have little experience or a lack of role models to show them how.

One sunny day, when I was out in my 1978 Toyota Cressida, I noticed the needle on the gas gauge was too low for me not to fill up. I would always drive it as far as I could and fill it up only when I could foresee myself having to push it soon.

I didn't have many assets when I left the house, but my father did buy me a car, so I at least had some transportation. I promised to pay back half the note when I got on my feet financially.

Making the tough decision that it was finally time to spend a few dollars on gas, I pulled into the Winn-Dixie. I checked my funds at the ATM to learn I had exactly $92.78 to my name. I let out a sigh but knew it was better than nothing.

Then I noticed one of those bank bags lying next to the ATM. It didn't look empty; it looked full. And the only thing that could be inside one of those bags was money. That seemed a little too good to be true, and my inner voice said, "*Do not* touch that bag."

While that seemed smart, I looked back at the number $92.78 on the screen and thought that anything more than that measly amount would be better. I had heard of people getting rewarded for turning in something valuable that had been lost.

So, against my better judgement, I picked it up. My body filled with fear. I looked to the left to see if anyone was around. Nobody. I looked to the right because somebody had to be watching, but nobody was.

I was frozen about what to do next, but it turned out that I did not have to make that decision. Two professionally dressed black women walked right up to me. Ooh, they smelled so good like perfume, and their lipstick was perfect. Their skirted suits fit them so well that I instantly trusted them. They looked so high caliber; they had to be trustworthy!

"What's wrong?" one of them asked.

Feeling like they could help, I answered, "I found this bag, and I think there's money inside. I don't know what to do."

She smiled and said, "Let's take it inside and have a closer look."

I waited in the parking lot while they went in. I should have run away, but I was still curious and hopeful for a piece of the pie. To my surprise, they came back out with the bag.

"We're going to take this to the police station. What's your name?" One of them asked.

"Natatia," I spilled.

"Okay, Natatia, you ride with me, and Belinda will follow us in the other car. Hop in the back."

Gulp. What did I just do? Oh, Lord, what was happening? I was terrified about what might happen if I got in the car with this lady. Why did we need to drive somewhere else? Were we really going to the police station? Would I make it back alive?

That was the instant I realized they were not trustworthy. The vibe they gave off was no longer kind or helpful. It started to feel horrible and scary. In a way, they made me feel like my mother did. I realized that they wanted to be in control, and I'd better do what they told me to.

Right before I think I blacked out (because the time in that woman's car was such a blur except for fear and perfume), I decided to play their game to survive. That's right. I plastered on my smile and went with it. I figured since they knew my name, they had me, and I would be better off acquiescing.

We did not go to the police station. We went back to the Winn-Dixie as my driver told me there was still some money left in the bathroom, and we should go get it. But first, I had to go back to the ATM and give them my last $92.78. I held back the tears as I drained my bank account and handed it to those women.

"You go in and get the rest from the bathroom, Natatia," Belinda directed. If that was even her real name. "We'll wait out here."

I bet you can imagine I was not surprised to find no money in the bathroom, and even less surprised to see that by the time I came out, the women were gone. Both their cars too. But they left the money bag.

They took all my money but left the bag. So I pulled back the zipper and peeked inside to find it full of meticulously folded newspaper.

The Lord's hammer just whacked me on the head.

I was duped. I felt so stupid that whole time, and this was why! But for some reason, I could not help but laugh. I just experienced a terrifying situation with strangers, and I was now broke.

But I was alive. I felt like an absolute idiot for not trusting my instincts when I first saw that bag, but I was alive. And hopefully smarter.

It took a while for me to forgive myself after that. I was naïve at nineteen, but that experience taught me a lot about trust:

- If something seems too good to be true, it probably is—especially in a situation as seemingly random as that.
- Trust your instincts. People give off a certain feeling or vibe when they interact with you. This vibe shows you their intention. Whether they are conscious of it or not, you can pick up on their intention beyond their words, dress, smell, or anything they might be using to trick you, if you pay attention to how they are making you feel under it all.
- If you ever get into a dangerous situation, focus on living instead of dying. I knew I wanted to live once I sat in the backseat of that car. So I played their game. I don't know if that's the only thing I could have done, but it was the tool I chose from my belt. And it helped me make it through because that was my focus.
- Forgive yourself as you learn. I was so mad that I fell for that money bag trick, but I later learned that it was a common trick at the time. Those women turned out to be professionals, but they were professional crooks!

- Find the lesson. We're not perfect, and we're always learning. But things really do happen to show us what we need to learn. My mother always said, "A bought lesson is better than a told one," meaning an experience that costed you money, pain or pride will teach you more than hearing advice from your parents, teachers, friends, etc. When you experience a lesson to the core, you (hopefully) will not get yourself into that situation ever again.

Now here's another way I learned not to trust others—even people that were close to me.

I don't know how she did it, but my mother would always squirrel information out of me. She would make me feel comfortable just long enough to extract personal thoughts like what happened at school that day, or what dreams I had for myself or how I felt about somebody else. And then, when she needed to one-up me for control, she would use that information against me!

This manipulation technique is known as "one-upmanship." The Oxford Advanced American Dictionary defines this as: "the technique or practice of gaining a feeling of superiority over another person" (Oxford Learner's Dictionaries, n.d.)

It was a technique! A practice! Well, let me tell you, my mother had this down to a science. Through all the times she simply berated the rest of my family members, she still knew she needed bait. She would lure me into a rare moment of security when we would talk about my life, my thoughts, my feelings. And she would just listen—quoting each word in the chalkboard of her mind, so she could use it later to cut me down.

Knowing she could do this so easily, and after experiencing it with others, I decided not to tell anyone anything. It was as if life was always handing me my Miranda rights saying that anything I say now can and will be used against me later.

Because it was.

So I stopped expressing how I felt, what I experienced and what I thought. And since nobody (except my husband now) could see behind my smile, nobody knew when I was suffering. I feel fortunate to have my husband as someone I can trust and talk to, and I'm working with my therapist to focus on finding and connecting with other people I can reach out to.

Having these people in our lives makes all the difference. Ask yourself if you have people you can talk to about anything without having it thrown back in your face. Ask the little people in your life if they have this. Ask your friends and family members.

I'm not suggesting that you be this person for them, unless you have the capacity, but it's good to open that conversation to make sure others around you can express themselves. It takes a little bit of trust to tell someone the small things, but it takes a huge amount to tell someone the big things, and as you can tell from reading the abusive stories people might have, we all need at least one person to share those big feeling and stories with.

4

Complex Post-Traumatic Stress Disorder

Most people have heard of post-traumatic stress disorder, or PTSD. While PTSD stems from an *event* like an accident, an injury, or witnessing someone's death, complex PTSD is caused by long-term submersion in a situation like growing up in an abusive household, being held somewhere dangerous against your will or enduring slavery.

If you know anybody who is easily set off by PTSD, you may understand how a triggering event, no matter how benign it seems to some people, can drop a normal person to their knees, send them into hiding or leave them in a crying fit.

My triggers occurred every day I taught school. You see, as a teacher, each day felt unpredictable like my childhood used to be. Not knowing what circumstance could cause my mother's volatile state to explode had me living in a state of anxiety, fearful of what was around the next corner.

As a teacher with twenty or more students in each class, I had this same sense. At any moment, one of those innocent children could be triggered from their own challenging life. I would always do whatever I could to help because, like I said earlier, I was the child whisperer. But sometimes I could not fully help because I was triggered myself and would go into a panic attack.

So little Jimmy is on the playground screaming that his life doesn't matter, and he's going to end it. Sweet Sofia just came out of the locker because a group of girls shoved her in it before the last class. Class clown Darin just learned his daddy went to jail that day.

I knew how these kids felt. But not only did I know, I could *feel* it all the way through my bones. My breath stopped. My heart raced. My blood pressure spiked. My vision went dark. I would try so hard to support that child—no matter who it was—but I was fighting for my own consciousness.

Their triggers became my triggers. And those triggers caused my panic attacks all too often in school. But let me tell you, I was so good at acting through these that most of the time nobody even knew what was happening to me; they were focused on me helping the child. I don't know how many times I acted my way through those scenes, but I thought I at least deserved to be nominated for an Emmy.

Nobody could hide behind that painted smile quite like I could.

Until I couldn't.

The day my blood pressure got above 160 (stroke level), the school secretary had to drive me to the emergency room. My husband met me there. I had a lot going on in my personal life, and to put a child's trauma on top of it spiraled me out of control.

In the hospital they helped me stabilize, but my cover was blown at the school. I had shown my own weakness. Hit the bottom of that barrel. I refused to succumb to my past fighting with my present (and even my future) on a daily basis.

So the next day I signed up for therapy.

Let me just pause here and point something out. In my childhood days, in my neighborhood, therapy made a person look incompetent at best. My mother refused and still refuses therapy. Though I was having two panic attacks a week during my teaching career, it took the one when I almost lost the fight before I decided to get help. I finally realized that if I didn't, I would not be able to help anyone anymore because I would not be here.

And I knew I was destined for more.

If you or anybody you know is having any level of anxiety, especially panic attacks, I want you to know that seeking help may be the key to not only saving but improving their life. If I can do it, you can do it.

If you can clear your trauma with guidance and supportive people around you, you are winning. I applaud you.

I eventually had to go on antidepressants because I was still too easily triggered. I entered cognitive behavior therapy and absorbed constant doses of positivity to help keep me on the right path forward. The loving support of my father was also imperative in keeping my soul inflated.

I was lucky to seek and find help. I feel fortunate to have come such a long way since those earlier teaching days. But I really had to get that diagnosis of CPTSD before I, and even other people in my life, could really take my healing journey seriously.

Many people who live with PTSD of any kind do the best they can to avoid their triggers altogether. Then they don't have to feel the anxiety creep in. It's painful and often embarrassing to find ourselves in that fight or flight moment, especially when people watch our unusual reactions and deem us odd.

Remember that story about the two women at Winn-Dixie? It took years before I could trust anyone who dressed professsionally, wore that same perfume or had the same shade of lipstick. This might seem overboard, but it's another example of how people hold trauma from certain aspects (words, smells, visuals, sounds, etc.) of their terrifying experiences.

But just like most neurological disorders, there are signs. Please be thoughtful as you read these. If they make you think of someone in particular, write their name down as you read. You might want to approach them later. If they make you think of yourself, talk to somebody you trust.

People with PTSD might:

- Begin to isolate themselves from normal daily activities at home, school or work, so they do not get triggered publicly. Even if they tell you they are okay, listen for the strength in their voice as they try to convince you. How convincing does their voice sound?
- Try to hide their depression behind a constant smile or empty eyes. Look into that person's eyes. Is there a blank stare in their pupils, or will they let you in? They might also cry much more often than most people, or they might not cry at all.
- Feel so empty inside that they have no energy to do anything. This can also result from the exhaustion someone lives through when consistently pretending or avoiding.
- Have no appetite at all, signaling a lack of desire to live. Or they might overeat to compensate for the emptiness inside. They might also overdo other things like exercise, shopping, drinking, etc. Again, watch for changes in habits.

You can also simply pay attention to friends or loved ones you have not seen in a while. Just reach out and ask how they are doing. It's possible for you to save someone's life by sending them a lifeline. Also, if you keep thinking of somebody, they flash through your mind or come to you in a dream, reach out then too. They could be asking for help in their own loneliness and the universe is summoning you.

Sometimes, however, that person in need *is* you. It's hard to recognize these attributes because you are the one experiencing them, not observing them, and you're often in denial or survival mode. I know I was.

If you want to find out how you are doing, here is one of the practices I did.

Sit yourself in front of a mirror and ask yourself, "Do I feel seen?" Answer it honestly and notice what comes up if you do not agree with the statement. Then ask, "Do I feel heard?" and answer honestly in the same way.

"Do I matter?" Ooh, pay special attention to what hits you when you ask that. If you don't answer with a resounding, "Yes, I do!" then you might have some work to do.

Lastly, ask yourself if you like what you see. If you want further confirmation, ask someone who loves you unconditionally to tell you what they see when they look at you or think of you.

Finding ways to better manage PTSD is on the forefront of science and psychology these days. But while having the possibility for better management and possibly a cure is deeply encouraging, we must first diagnose it. The more you can pay attention to others who might have the behaviors described above, the more of a chance you can give someone, or yourself, to enjoy a more normal and meaningful life.

Part 2

Rising

This section is where we really begin to see hope. To believe there is light at the end of the dismal tunnel.

People who survive trauma have pain, but over time, that pain turns to scars. The scars are not only reminders of what we have been through, but proof of what we can endure. And it might be surprising what kind of tools those scars can turn into.

There is a lot of work to be done from this point on, but having the guidance, hope and support to carry on makes all the difference. No matter what role you have in this journey, I hope you find support as you forge ahead.

5

Survival Mechanisms

Victims of trauma do not solely pack their bags with painful memories and emotional layers—they leave a little room for tools. A victim, by definition, can only be a victim in the moment they are tormented. Once the storm is over, and they are still alive, they are called survivors and witnesses.

But how does a person come out of such turbulence and carry on? There's an alchemy that happens in the brain to help a person find their strength to move forward. This can be in the form of learned or unconscious survival mechanisms. If this didn't happen, that victim would not emerge as a survivor.

Here are some of the methods I used to continue to crawl out of my storm toward a better life. While there can be an array of others depending on a person's innate capabilities, these are widely adopted throughout society, and most genuine for me to speak about. These methods include:

- Faith in a higher power
- Resilience and determination
- Masking with a smile

I feel so blessed that I had a fire inside me to keep going, healing and growing. While these methods conjure more positivity than the effects mentioned in the previous chapter, an extreme use of them can also be signs that someone is clinging to their buoy extra tight to stay afloat. Pay attention to inflated versions of these methods as signs of overcompensation and red flags that someone still needs help.

Faith in a Higher Power

We all have our story of how religion or spirituality shaped our upbringing. And quite often, the role spirituality played while we were highly moldable evolves—as we grow, have conflicting experiences and ask questions.

Whatever your journey, I hope you get to a place where you find peace in your heart and purpose in your soul—no matter who, where or what it comes from.

My first experiences with faith and religion were fragmented. My father loved to visit his childhood church with his mother and grandmother. I could tell this was important to him. He even became an ordained minister after he divorced my mother years later.

But as a family, we never went to church. By my mother's hand, we were not allowed. Although I never asked her questions about this for fear her answers would sting as much as her own experience did, I figured religion in some way caused her pain too. Perhaps she had reasons to be mad at God. Maybe she felt betrayed.

All I knew was that Sunday was the day my father often left to go to church with his family in another town, and the day my mother would be most volatile—almost like the devil himself would rise through her. I still shudder to think of that now.

Though I did not understand all the teachings from the gospel or Bible, I picked up enough bits and pieces to find my own image of who God was to me: a protector, a provider and someone who watched over us. I was comforted by the notion that there was an entity powered by benevolence to help keep the world together. I started having hope that God would help save us when my own world felt like it was falling apart.

To supplement what I heard, I did my own reading to learn that kindness could get me into Heaven, and the Devil would take me away if I was mean to my siblings. Boy, did my imagination run wild with those stories!

I also believed in other spiritual beings as I could see illuminations around people. And to this day, I believe in miracles.

My foundation seemed innocent and hopeful.

But let me tell you, when I was stuck in my house day after day, night after night with a woman who was just trying to keep us contained and "protected," I seriously began to question God's love and protection. The abuse escalated as we grew older, and my life rarely felt like it was mine to experience. I felt trapped and abandoned. I grew angry and confused. I would look out my window and argue, "Why God? Why do you let this happen?"

This was a pivotal time in my own evolution with faith. I felt so betrayed that I felt I had two options. One was to turn away from faith entirely (like my mother probably did—I could see why she did it). The other was to dig deeper to find a meaning to make sense of my world.

My questions could not be quelled either way, and I eventually realized that I could not revere God as an entity distant from myself. The more I let God be an ever-present force, the more I was able to take responsibility for my decisions and the consequences. I was also able to surrender my questions, doubts and anger to God, learning that, in doing so, I felt momentarily liberated. Soon enough it seemed that answers, faith and peace would come back around to reveal themselves.

Oh, what a journey. This is sometimes the most important, messy, and all-consuming journey of a person's life. I can testify to that.

But I still had my intuition that would speak louder and louder. When I listened, things turned out okay. When I didn't, like the story about the money bag, things went awry really fast. I felt like the more I paid attention to these feelings, the more I was being led to the right path and to the next part of the journey that just might have a little light at the end.

Beyond this, I started to notice synchronicities in my life—events that felt like divine messages or affirmations. After reading the book by SQuire Rushnell, I continue to call them God Winks. By paying attention to what seems like coincidences, you may find that you are on the right path too. Some examples of God Winks may include:

- Unexpected timing: Running into an old friend just when you were thinking about them.
- Affirmation or guidance: Seeing a specific sign, number, or word that aligns perfectly with what you were praying about or considering.
- Encouragement: Receiving a solution or opportunity that directly responds to your struggles or questions.

This term is rooted in the idea that there are no coincidences, only moments orchestrated by a higher power to remind you of God's presence, love, and guidance. It's often associated with feelings of comfort, clarity, and reassurance.

Currently, my husband and I are Eucharistic Ministers visiting the sick and homebound parishioners after church each Sunday. It's meaningful to us both, just like it was to my father.

I know that faith can differ from person to person, but one thing that remains strong throughout any belief system is that choosing kindness is always the best answer. When I do this, my own path gets brighter. To live in service to others and always be searching for the path that feels right is the most neutral advice I can give—and anyone can do it.

While faith in a guiding light or a divine feeling is normal and healthy for many people, the overcompensation of this would look quite obvious. Someone who is using religion or spirituality as their only lifeline might make them look like a martyr in daily life. They might be making all their decisions based on what God wants them to do or isolating themselves from previous activities because it now makes them feel like a heathen.

Condescending behavior toward people with differing beliefs can be a sign of this also. An unhealthy spiritual or religious zest begins with polarization and can surmount to a more radical and condemning approach toward others. Some people may use their new faith to be their sole reason for living, which can also cause a disconnection down the line.

Resilience and Determination

As we touched on earlier, when people are constantly told "no" to their desires, they usually react one of two ways: they cower and truly believe they have no freedom, or they rebel. The survivor will choose rebellion, and this rebellion, once paired with grace, becomes resilience and determination. It can be the reason a person believes in themselves for the rest of their life. It can become the spark that triggers them to become stronger, try harder and make their beliefs a priority.

They want to prove the naysayer wrong.

It's obvious I chose this path, and I chose it hard. Not only did I want to prove my mother wrong for everything she told me I could not do, but I also wanted to go beyond negating that to prove to myself I could do even better. I attended so much school that I achieved my All But Dissertation (ABD) and earned my Educational Specialist (Ed.S.) degree in Teacher Leadership in

2005. Then I earned Educational Leadership credentials while teaching full-time.

One day I asked myself, "Why do I need to keep proving myself enough?" And when I really dug for the answer, it was simple: a fancy title does not define who I am or the legacy I will leave. My inner shine and how I helped humanity in this lifetime is what matters.

Let that woman tell me I don't want to be a teacher now!

But while resilience and determination can be powerful tools for helping us succeed on the path of life, overachieving is a sign that we are trying to compensate for the unworthiness in our past. My therapist pointed this out.

The little voice in my brain that always tried to prove my mother wrong escalated as my success in education and leadership grew. As a Black woman, I often felt overlooked in leadership spaces, which at times threw me into the patterns I learned in my childhood.

Through therapy and self-advocacy, I finally realized I did not need validation from others; however, that took years and I'm still working on it. I also no longer feel like I must be the best or shine in every moment, but I do like to leave a shine behind once I leave the room.

It's healthy to want to succeed. If you believe that you can do something wonderful, do it! The world needs that! I encourage you to tap in to your passions and align your actions with your values to overcome any feelings of inadequacy.

But striving to hit the next notch without acknowledging your previous success suggests you may want to look deeper to find out what you are compensating for. Once you can clear the hurt from your past, you will see you have so much more to give.

Masking with a Smile

Let's face it, this works… at least for a while.

If we can keep a smile on during our current hardships while hiding the ones from our past, we almost become invisible. We become that person that nobody checks on because we seem to be doing just fine. People don't often worry about the person who seems to have their life together. They worry and reach out to the people who don't.

But this can't last forever. If you are overdoing the smile in every moment like I was, either you need to change best friends regularly, or you will soon get questioned. And good on that friend who makes a bold move by prying you out of your comfort zone because they noticed you were not really all that comfortable in the first place.

We can fake our way through the grocery store. We can smile our time away at a party. We can mask up at work. But eventually, something will crack. It will either be us, or it will be that person who cares about us enough to see this as a façade.

Like I said, I would smile and laugh while I was bullied in school. Not only did this prove to the bully that I was not affected by their antics, it gave me time to think. My smile closed the curtain over my feelings, so the behind-the-scenes action could take place. Next time I acted, I was going to be in another scene, and that scene would be under my direction.

This technique worked for me so well that I started flaunting it! Have you seen these pearly whites? Well, you will because they pop behind the red wine lipstick I wear. If my smile is going to get me through most of my days, then you better believe I designed that stage for success.

But now you know my secret. And it is honestly a tactic many other people use, so if you are that friend who cares about someone whose smile looks more like a puppet show, please ask them about it. A true friend might really appreciate it. Goodness knows they need it.

And if you can't be the one to ask, find somebody else they trust.

6

Breaking Generational Cycles

Generational cycles are patterns that get repeated and passed down from parents to children over and over again. They can be like a tradition, but often unconscious and emotionally based.

When parents lack the tools to observe, control and repair their own unfavorable behaviors, they unconsciously show their children negative ways adults can behave. But worse than this, since it is so consistent and fundamental to the household, it is often deemed as acceptable.

When a child sees this behavior day after day and year after year, they will most likely conclude that that is how life is. That it's the way to parent. Yes, they may take on the pain and scars mentioned in the previous chapters, but they also might think that is simply the way a parent behaves.

What happens if this remains untreated and misunderstood?

When that child has a family, they will most likely do the same thing to their children causing that generational cycle to continue.

After seeing what I have seen in the school system as an educator and being raised the way I was, I think there should be mandatory therapy sessions and even a test people should endure before they can raise children of their own. These cycles could be stopped before they start if the potential parents healed their wounds and understood how to nurture children amidst life's struggles.

But who am I to make this a requirement? God had other plans for me, and I was never able to have children of my own. However, I always promised that if I did, I would raise them better than my mother raised us.

Rooted in Control and Survival

My mother rarely spoke of her upbringing, so I don't have many clues as to how her parents were raised (taking the generational cycle back another round), but I know enough about how she was raised.

Her father, my grandfather, ruled the house with an iron fist. Oh, he was *mean*! Well, at least my mother portrays him that way. And my grandmother, her mom, was largely silent about what happened in the household. Probably similar to how my father protected my mother's vehemence.

And while my mother could have taken on her own feminine role of being quiet and subservient, she ended up donning her father's iron glove and trying to dictate every aspect of our lives.

My mother's parents died when she was a teenager. She had ten brothers and two sisters to contend with. I would like to say they all worked together to survive, but living lives ruled by strict control and hardship did not give them the tools for this. It made them grasp for whatever they *could* control and fear the rest.

My mother, as one of the few females, also had to fend off predatory men—some who she could not escape proximity from. She learned to trust no one. She learned that all men only want one thing. She learned that the only way she could feel safe was to control everything she could that was happening around her.

Can you see why she raised us the way she did? She didn't know any better! Her perception of the world shaped her reality, and the only way she knew how to navigate involved manipulation and fear.

Let's also consider the fact that, since her parents were not around the whole time, she had to fend for herself, living in fear. So the way she had to control every aspect of our lives could also be because she thought she was protecting us. But we were "protected," not nurtured, and this left no room for trust, freedom or emotional connection to bloom.

The emotional impact my siblings and I received from our mother was largely shaped by her wounds. They were still open, weeping and bleeding. She felt she had no control over her past, so all her control wrapped around us as if we could be her bandage.

Many critical relationships we as adolescents could have had were overshadowed by her need for control. Our whereabouts and choices were on her radar and tight leash. I felt unseen and unheard because my desires did not seem to matter or got quickly extinguished. That's why I had to hide so much of my life from her.

Like my first steady boyfriend.

He was a handsome football player and luckily, he was a friend of the family, so he already knew of my mother's mental illness… and that she usually carried a weapon of choice.

One day, he came over to our house while our mother was at work. We were all used to sneaking people around, but on this particular day, she pulled into the driveway during her lunch break.

"Quick! In the closet!" I cried as my brother and sister helped stuff him in the hallway closet. Ooh, it was going to be hot in there, but we could not risk our mother seeing a boyfriend visiting with-out her permission. Especially a boyfriend she didn't know about!

"Don't you say a word until we let you out!" I demanded through the keyhole as my mother's car door slammed.

"And don't sneeze!" my sister added.

"Or fart!" my brother snickered.

But as our mother turned the doorknob to the front door, our faces became stoic. We hid behind our plastered smiles and acted as if nothing was going on. Nothing to hide. Nothing to find here.

At one point our mother was standing right next to the closet door, just cursing up a storm. I could feel little sweat beads on my hairline. If we had not been so good at hiding behind our masks, I'm not sure any of us could have pulled this off.

I secretly wondered how my beau was doing in that tiny, hot closet with her shouting just two feet away. He was probably sweating more than the rest of us combined. But if any of us would have led on in the tiniest way, there would have been an instant interrogation followed by punishment. And I prayed behind my eyes that the harmless boy in the closet would escape with all his limbs.

I don't know how we managed, but nearly an hour later she left, and we opened the door to that closet triumphantly. For a young man who was sitting on a bucket hanging on to a broom handle, he sure looked exhausted. And as hot as he was, he was afraid to come out.

"Are you sure she's gone?" he asked twice before he would even budge.

There is something to be said about understanding the intentions of another person. If I would have had a boyfriend from a different school who didn't know my mother, he may have gotten too hot, figured the discomfort wasn't worth it after twenty minutes and popped out for fresh air not understanding the risk of being shot at.

But my hunky football player? He put all his effort into survival. Just like my mother did growing up.

Her unhealed pain not only affected her family, but anyone who dared to enter her house.

My Vow to Break this Cycle

Being the rebellious, overachieving woman that I am, I was not left in the dark about how I was parented. I knew better than to raise a child the way we were brought up.

But deep down I questioned my ability to be a mother without replicating the harmful patterns I experienced. Could I do it better, or was I destined to continue the cycle? For years, I told myself I'd rather not have children than perpetuate the same pain and control that defined my upbringing.

My body not only heard me say this, it manifested my wish that I'd rather not have children if I would be the same kind of mother. After I started talking to my therapist, however, I was able to turn this doubt around and make a vow: if I ever *did* have children, I would break that cycle.

Instead of doubting my abilities, I began working on myself and believing that I was healed and strong enough to be a loving, nurturing, understanding parent. And together with my sweet husband, we embarked on this journey in hopes that I could prove it.

But after all those years cursing my body along with the Lord's plan for me, we realized I would never get to be a mother to a child of my own. That arduous journey could be a book in itself, but I do have proof that my siblings are capable of this as I watch my sister with her daughter.

My sister treats her daughter just the way I promised I would treat a child of my own, and this brings me great comfort to know that healing and change are possible in the face of deeply engrained patterns.

I give a lot of credit to my sister for being able to do this. She probably worked as hard as I did to get to that place.

So, while I can't prove it's possible through myself, I can show you through my kin. And that is enough to break this cycle.

As this book is written, my mother is still alive. And wouldn't you know it, she does not agree with the way my sister raises her daughter. Mother thinks they are too much like friends when my sister should have more power and control over her daughter. Well my mother did not get therapy, and at this point, she will probably remain just as she was until her time on this earth is done. But we can see how she got to be that way.

The rest of my living family offers a legacy of protection to each other and our descending generations, no matter how they emerge. As we discuss our upbringing, there is still a lot of pain that comes up, but we all understand and offer a safe place to reflect. And though our mother is still capable of inflicting pain, we do our best to shield against it.

Our goal now is to protect each other and be better for the future.

Signs Someone is Hurting

People who are hurting from emotional wounds past and present often act in harmful ways to others. It's as if they are trying to project their pain onto others, but often, they don't even know they are doing this.

Here are some common signs to look for in someone who may have wounds that need healing:

- Control as a defense mechanism. A person may attempt to control every aspect of their environment because, as we saw with my mother, it helps them feel safe even when it causes harm to others. When a student, loved one or stranger lashes out or appears not to be teachable, they are actually trying to control each piece of the situation as a defense mechanism.

- Projecting pain. When people lash out through passive aggressive or aggressive behavior, they are usually unable to process emotions in healthy ways. When I left home, I was wounded. I made a vow not to project pain onto others, but it did come out occasionally. Both types of behaviors may emerge when the hurting person is seemingly unprovoked, but we do not always know someone's triggers. When these behaviors show up in the classroom, on the playground or in work environments, gently ask the person questions when they are calm. They may need help getting out of their own emotional cycle.
- Fear-based parenting. As I witness parents in the school system, this can look like over-protection of the child, harsh discipline and/or micromanagement, which stifles the child's ability to grow and thrive. They may also blame the school system for their child's behavior. The child may also act differently around the parent—this could show up in a variety of dynamics, but the main point is that they are acting noticeably different or suspicious when the parent is watching.
- Emotional unavailability. I also like to call this emotional constipation because our emotions get *stuck*. A hurting person might struggle to connect to someone else emotionally, leading to relationships that feel cold, aloof or distant. This was me even after I left home. It was not until I met my husband that I could give someone a genuine hug. Now my whole family gives hugs thanks to him opening that door.

The important thing to note here is that these parents, neighbors, loved ones—whoever they may be to us—are stuck in emotional pain. We can't just label them as bad people. We must show empathy, and try to get them help, so they don't hurt their children or other people. This cycle will perpetuate itself if we deal with hurting people in the same way they were dealt with in the first place.

We must see the bigger picture and take a stronger, more empathetic role. This is how we help break the cycle for them.

Choosing Healing Over Hurt

Breaking generational cycles is a conscious and continuous decision. Simply proclaiming that we want to break the cycle is not enough. The choices made in each moment, especially regarding emotions and triggers, must be intentional and consistent.

Just as it is true for changing any habit, this is most difficult at first. Like getting a rusty wheel to turn. Many parts of our darkest stored emotions will show up when we did not even realize they existed. We will be met with surprises, bumps and curves, often discouraging us.

But we must keep trying.

As our road to recovery smooths out, it becomes more like maintenance. Our knee-jerk reactions become positive because we have worked to reinforce and change the behavior.

Change is possible.

My sister is doing it with her daughter. When becoming a parent, she took a step back, analyzed what she liked and disliked about her own upbringing, and chose the best path forward for her family. She chooses understanding over fear. Love over control. Empowerment over dominance.

Their relationship has become a beacon for the rest of our family to convey that the past does not have to define the future. With the exception of my mother, of course, we are all so proud of our sister.

As for me, I have been in therapy for eleven years and counting to process what I have experienced. And now, after looking back and being able to see things with a wider scope, I can see that this is the only way forward. I am now responsible for imparting this knowledge through my own behavior, but even more, I choose to look for these signs in others.

Many of the signs listed above are plain to see in another person. I would imagine that you can think of several people right now who are hurting. Take a moment to assess the attributes they possess and decisions they make that portray this.

Now, instead of judging them, or putting them in a box as someone who may never change, offer them empathy.

You can do this quietly in your mind as you meditate, pray or daydream, or you can initiate a conversation with them. Tell them that you see their pain, and they are not alone. Let them know that help is available if they wish to change their own cycles and life. If they choose to change their patterns, they will also change their relationships for the better. This becomes a side effect of feeling better about yourself. When you have respect for yourself, you will more easily respect others, inviting them to hold respect for you.

Think about it. If we are conscious enough to look beyond someone's words and peer into their soul, we can see what is happening. We can empathize. We can spark a change.

Yes, we can choose healing over hurt for ourselves, but we can also help facilitate this in each other, with no special tools or education—just love and compassion.

You don't have to understand what someone else is going through to offer them these gifts. Learning from my own experience, sometimes all a person needs is to see proof—even in someone else—that change is possible.

And we can do this for every single person on the planet.

7

Empathy

I learned empathy from watching people's unsaid words. I learned this mainly from my mother because she never seemed to mean the things she said. Even as a young girl I realized that people do not always say what they really mean. I felt that, if this was truly the case, conversations would be pointless. I became determined to find a better way to read somebody, so I could find a way out of this confusion.

I found that if I turned my ears off, I could get a clearer picture of what a person meant underneath what they were saying. The way my mother would hover over me to look taller, lean forward to intimidate me, use large gestures for power and gaze daggers into my eyes showed me that she was trying to keep me submissive. It didn't even matter what she was saying—her goal was to maintain control over me… and my entire family.

Some of the teachers at school, and that custodian I adored, would smile with a soft look in their eyes. They would kneel down to get at eye level with the students. Their shoulders would be relaxed, and their gestures would be soft. I learned that these mannerisms, especially when used in combination, signaled respect and appreciation toward others.

Empathy as a Gift

I will be honest and say that for much of my childhood, I did not really hear much of what adults said. I was too busy reading between the lines, trying to *feel* their intentions. I carried this on because it seemed so natural and effective.

It was mildly confusing for me at first, but I eventually got used to it. And now that I'm an adult, I can see how this intentional behavior is unfolding in miraculous ways.

I no longer focus solely on people's body positions and gestures. I look into their eyes. When I look into someone's eyes with curiosity, empathy and love, I can see into their soul. I can see what they might not even know is there.

Like my mother's pain.

All the emotions people feel emit a vibration, and whether we know it or not, an empath can feel that. Your emotion becomes a vibe to an empath, so pay attention to yourself! You are not keeping any secrets!

When I walk into a room, I can feel the vibe so well that I am guided on where to take my seat. I will not sit until the air around me feels clear. So sometimes I just stay standing!

The more my intuitions are correct, the more I believe in them, and the more confident I feel about listening. The more I have something to trust and believe in, the stronger I become.

Even when my instincts frighten me.

Remember "the glow" I saw around my father the day I felt those scars on his back for the first time? I see that in others too. It's a lovely golden glow surrounding a person, making their skin look radiant and sun-kissed. Though aesthetically this vision is pleasing to my eye, its meaning is often foreboding.

The last time I saw my grandpa-in-law Dun Dun at Thanksgiving, he was a bit cranky, when usually he was even-keeled. But as I looked at him without judgement across the table, I nearly choked on a bite of turkey. "Oh, my God. He has the look!" I whispered behind my napkin. Knowing that this enlightenment was not a dinner discussion, I kept it to myself. What would my family say anyway?

Dun Dun died two weeks later.

I see this glow in others. A bit more than I would like. When I see this around a person when it does not make any sense, I can't even look them in the eyes. The glow around them is so burdensome that it keeps me from looking into their soul. And I do not dare to tell anybody in the moment.

For a while, I called myself the Queen of Death. But as time went on, I realized this glow did not always mean death, it sometimes just meant a peaceful transition in this life or to the next. That was a relief because I also began to think of this ability as a curse. Why should I be the one to have this information? What a heavy gift!

Now I see this as part of being an empath. I also see it as one of my gifts. And no matter how disturbing or mystical our gifts may seem, we have them for a purpose. Pay attention to your gifts and use them for good in the world. Not everyone can do what you do.

How to Learn Empathy

Can you imagine what the world would be like if we were all able to look into each other's souls without judgement? If we could see that most people are in pain and all they need is love and connection? We would not be able to hurt another soul because we could already see they are as wounded as we are.

Is it possible for us to live in a world like this?

I would like to think so.

That's why I want to share a simple technique to start you on your journey of helping to promote empathy, compassion and understanding in this world.

But first, I have a quick question for you. Why do we get so mushy over babies and puppies? How can a person who can barely look their own family in the eye so easily lose themselves in the face of a cute baby or a fluffball of a pup?

Is it simply because they are adorable?

Not entirely.

Babies, puppies, kitties—and honestly, most animals that are not afraid of you or want to eat you—are curious about their surroundings. They observe without judgement. They let you in when they look back at you, and they let you in *just as you are.*

They reflect your innocence and light. For some of us, it's the only time we feel accepted just as we are, so we tend to linger as long as we can.

So let's practice this technique on babies and innocent animals. It is a safe place to start. If you don't have easy access to these beings, go to a pet store or animal shelter. The neighbor's house. The park. Anywhere you might find these powerful life forces.

If you cannot find real souls close by, find a picture online or maybe even from your past. Using a picture of a being that is staring innocently, directly into the camera, is better than nothing at all.

This is what we are going to practice: staring into their eyes.

At first when you do this, notice the thoughts that come to your mind. Notice them without judgement to see where you currently stand. After you are aware of your comfort level of the situation, send intention.

Even if you do not speak the words (which can be moot anyway), direct thoughts of love into them. Through their eyes and into their soul. Imagine your thoughts of love settling right into their heart. You can send thoughts like:

I see you for who you are, and you're beautiful.

No matter what, you are loved.

You are a gift to the world. Thank you for being here.

Next, observe how they send it back to you. Ooh, doesn't that feel good?

I do this with babies and animals all the time. They love me back, and that's because I love them first.

Next step: An adult.

First, figure out who you are more comfortable doing this with—yourself or a dear friend. If you have a friend you trust enough to do this with, you are already winning at life. If you don't and you think you can break through your own judgment of yourself and love yourself unconditionally, I commend you as well.

And if you are not ready for a real person, try a picture of someone who is gazing into the camera with love.

Repeat this, repeat this, repeat this. Do this every day. Once you move beyond the young and innocent, once you master your own reflection, once you are able to look into your friend's soul, you are ready to move on to the next level of people: strangers and acquaintances.

Look into people's eyes lovingly at work. When you go out to eat. Anywhere you feel comfortable making eye contact with people you know and even complete strangers.

When you are ready for the real challenge, do this with people who have previously wronged you (you might want to read the Forgiveness chapter first). Family members who you don't see eye to eye with. People you don't agree with. Anyone you feel triggered by or tend to judge.

Can you learn to look at them with love? Can you look into their soul and see that they are still hurting as a child and that is why they choose to hurt others? Can you do that?

What if we all could?

This is a huge step the world needs to take in order to heal. If we can look into everybody's—and I mean *every*body's—eyes, see their soul and send them love and compassion, we will make this world a better place.

We all need empathy. Some of us can feel it more than others, but if we all try, we will be in a much better place together.

8

Forgiveness

Forgiveness is not about erasing the past or pretending the pain didn't happen. It's about letting go of the hurt that holds us back—freeing ourselves to heal, grow, and embrace the light within ourselves that no one can dim without us allowing it.

I believe this to be true with all my heart. I am also living proof that it works. I would not even fathom writing this book if I had not done the work to forgive my mother and myself. And now that I have truly liberated myself from the anger, guilt and shame that came with it, I can see it all as part of the plan.

Throughout my whole life, I would tell myself, "I was made for more than this." More than an abusive household with no freedom. More than a technical school. More than a babysitter. The good Lord knows I have an impassioned spirit, so he made sure I could jump through all those flaming hoops before I decided to take a stand. If I would have had an easy life, how would I have earned this devotion to speak out? Why would I feel the need to educate educators? Why would I feel it's my duty to speak on stages and write a book to help others heal?

The truth is, I would not. The talents, insights and fervor I possess might have gone to waste.

But they will not.

The final and most harrowing hoops I found in this process were the hoops of forgiveness: one for my mother and one for me.

When we feel we have been wronged by another person, we often feel the need to keep judgement and blame on them for our entire lives. We may think something like, "That person hurt me, so they are bad, and I will be mad at them forever. That will show them!"

But what if I thought that about my mother? What if I still believed the tactics she used to make me feel small, unseen and unworthy were simply because she was evil? What if I decided to see her as such and punish her by holding on to that guilt, anger and shame?

Now I will say that I tried that for a while, but it had no effect on her.

Let me say that again.

All the anger and rage I hung onto for my mother had no effect on her.

And what really torched my hide, was that it had *all* the effect on me. I was only punishing myself, so I finally decided to try the forgiveness route.

After working on conquering that feat, I no longer believe there are bad people. Just bad cycles of pain, disconnection, fear and loneliness. When people act from these cycles, like my mother did, they do not really have any other options. It is not until a person steps out of their cycle and sees it for what it is, that they can also forgive and heal themselves.

My mother was and is not a bad person. She is hurting. I understand this, so I can genuinely publish this letter I wrote to her from my younger self.

Mother Dearest,

I see you.

I see the strength you carried, the battles you fought and the pain that shaped you. I understand that life wasn't easy for you and that your wounds may have influenced how you expressed love.

As a child, I longed for your affection, approval and gentle guidance. Instead, I often encountered harsh words and actions that left me feeling unworthy and unseen. Those experiences left scars, but they also ignited a fire within me—a determination to break the cycle and to heal.

Today, I choose forgiveness—not to excuse the pain but to release its hold on me. Forgiveness is my gift to myself, a declaration that past hurts no longer define me.

I have grown into a woman who embraces her worth, speaks her truth and offers compassion—even when it's difficult. I carry the lessons of the past not as burdens but as stepping stones toward a brighter future.

I hope we can one day share a space of mutual respect and understanding. Until then, I will continue to honor my journey and nurture the peace and joy I have cultivated.

With love and hope,

Little Natatia (Tomato)

It took a lot of therapy and prayer to get to that point of forgiveness. Once my therapist got me on the right track, I reminded myself of my new journey with the Lord's Prayer: "Forgive us our trespasses as we forgive those who trespass against us."

Forgiveness is not new. It's ancient. And it works.

But sometimes forgiving the other person can be the easy part. Remember I said sometimes. All situations are different.

I was always one to extend grace to others, but when it came to doing the same for myself, I did not think I deserved it. But I spent my childhood trying to survive in somebody else's cycle of pain and blame, so I did the best with what I knew.

All those times I felt guilty for not standing up to her when she cut me or other people down? That was not my duty, nor would it make her see the light. All those times I snuck out of the house for a date, a friend or a moment of freedom? I needed to experience some avenues of normalcy as an adolescent. The unjust acts I committed to get my peers to notice me and validate me? I never meant to hurt anyone, but I did not feel seen or validated at home. And all those times I lied and smeared a smile across my face pretending I was fine? I was afraid something terrible would happen if people knew the truth.

I could keep going, but this is not a confession booth. This is me sharing my examples with you, in hopes you can find the origins of the limiting beliefs you might be holding within yourself.

No matter what you are holding onto because you blame yourself, please know you can also liberate yourself from those shackles by realizing you did the best you could with what you knew and what you had at the time. If you (or I) would have known better, we probably would not have done those things in the first place.

Agreed?

Give yourself grace. Even I had to work at that.

I wish I could say that getting through forgiveness is as easy as jumping through a flaming hoop. But it's not. It's more like a flaming tunnel.

Once you start, you will spend a lifetime noticing things you have to forgive in others and yourself. And sometimes, the same person over and over. This can be daunting, let me tell you. But it is absolutely worth it.

I often remember the optimism of my father, and how it got me through so many hard times. I don't have many people I can think of who always looked at me like I was worth something, but he did. For that I am forever grateful because when I lose faith in myself to keep trudging forward, his genuine smile can show up in my memory and cheer me on.

Also, I've been cheering myself on for so long that I give a good high five to myself. Yes, it might look strange if someone catches me, but I am able to stay encouraged and stay proud of my progress.

My goal is for you to also see that each small act of forgiveness is a step toward healing and progressing toward your innate potential. Forgiving others frees our hearts to open toward love, and forgiving ourselves frees our souls to be our best selves.

If you're stuck in blame and shame, please ask someone to help guide you into forgiveness. There are so many practices and processes you can try to get this to work for you. As humans, we make mistakes, but holding on to that shame and blame keeps us small and heavy.

Choosing to forgive—whoever it may be—is the first and most powerful step. Continue your process until you can look back and say, "Oh, that's why that happened." You will see it as an incident separate from you, not who you are.

Part 3

Paths Forward

I am thrilled that you are still with me. And no matter who you are, this section is specifically designed for *you*. Which role do you play in this?

- If you have been abusive or hurtful to people you love, see Chapter 9.
- If you want to advocate for or help a loved one, coworker, neighbor, *any*one you think that is hiding behind their smile or pain, see Chapter 10.
- If you are currently living in fear or stuck in old patterns from past trauma, see Chapter 11.
- No matter who you are, end with Chapter 12.

Regardless of your current role, it would be beneficial to read each chapter. Walking in someone else's shoes is the best way to understand what they are going through and how to help either them or yourself.

This section is intended to offer insights and foster greater awareness of trauma, healing, and resilience. It is not a substitute for professional medical, psychological, or therapeutic advice, diagnosis, or treatment. Readers facing serious personal challenges are encouraged to seek assistance from qualified mental health professionals or licensed counselors.

The case studies presented in the following chapters are based on real-world scenarios but have been anonymized and fictionalized to protect the identities of individuals involved. They are included for illustrative purposes and should not be interpreted as direct representations of any specific person or family.

Let's dive in.

9

Hurting Others

Do You Identify?

In the past week or month or year, have you physically laid hands (or other body parts) on another person with the intention to harm or control? Have you used a weapon or your own power as a threat?

Have you used your own emotions, whether anger, guilt or shame with the intention to harm or control another person? Do you often say something you later regret to loved ones? Do you find it hard to control your anger? Do you often blame others because you don't see how something can be your fault?

When somebody does or says something, to you or someone else, that does not play out like you intended, do you stop the world from turning, make sure the spotlight is on you, and admonish the perpetrator?

Or do you ever just wonder why? *Why* am I doing these things to hurt other people?

If you can identify with most of these questions, then chances are you have some pain to work through in order to stop the cycle of hurting others. And as you continue to read this, I commend you with all my heart because this may be your first step to healing yourself and saving the ones you love.

I'm proud of you.

Validating Your Feelings

Chances are some of the tactics you use to control others (whether you know it or not), are from scenarios you have already experienced in your own life.

When you think back to your childhood, how do you feel? Do you get a sick feeling? Do you get angry? Do you want to block out the thought all together? It's possible that some of the people in your own childhood or throughout your life didn't always know how to treat you or others around you. If you are still holding on to pain, fear or trauma from experiences in your life, you may not have full respect for yourself, and in turn, you may have a hard time treating others with respect.

So sometimes you do things that hurt them.

Maybe with your body. Maybe with your words. Maybe by not acknowledging them at all. This may or may not be intentional.

If this describes how you feel about yourself or others, then please know that your reactions are normal; far too common, but normal.

Oftentimes, someone like yourself gets openly criticized, blamed or judged for your actions. In your defense, that will not help you open up to your own wounds and walk a journey of healing. You need a safe space where you are not criticized, blamed or judged. You may even have to remove yourself from the people that trigger you in order to find the strength to take that path forward.

Are you ready to feel better about yourself? Your actions? Your relationships? Do you want to believe there is a better life out there waiting for you?

Transformation to a brighter place is possible. When you can see that those things you experienced were simply experiences, and not the definition of who you are, you can learn to detach yourself from the pain caused by those events and start to see a lighter version of yourself.

How can you do that?

Steps Forward

Your first step is recognizing your actions are hurting others.

The second is wanting to change.

The next step is to surround yourself with people who believe in you. The past is done, and you can recreate your future anytime you want. If you do not have many people around who are willing or able to effectively accompany you on this journey, ask a trusted friend to help you find a professional setting or support group who can.

Remember, your goal here is to be able to assess how you are feeling in a judgment-free zone. When you are around the right people to assist with your healing, they will understand you because they may have been through it themselves. Finding a group like this is crucial.

And recognizing in others how change is possible is an impactful way to strike inspiration in your heart. Here are some support ideas to try if you are wondering where to start.

Journaling: Writing is not always an easy thing to do, but penning your thoughts into a journal is a safe place to put them. If you are worried about anybody else seeing it, you can hide it in between your vents. And I use the word vent to try to instill the fact that you are not necessarily trying to create or make up anything on the page; you are simply going to let it out of you. Vent it out of your being, so it sees the light of day in your book. Even if it's out only long enough for you to acknowledge what is written and see it for what it is: buried emotion.

The more you can write without judging yourself, without judging the emotions that express themselves or the way you word them, the more honestly they can flow out. You want the truth to come out. Take a deep breath and invite those feelings to emerge. Let it out, no matter how much it might scare you at first. Release it without judgment so it can escape your being. Then you can figure out what to do with what you learn.

Mantras: Once you identify what you have been holding on to and release it, you can choose how to refill that space. Do you want to keep telling yourself that you have been a horrible person? Do you want to remind yourself how ashamed you are?

No.

You did what you did because that's what you had the tools to do. To create some mantras (daily inspirational phrases), you need to know what you need to oppose. Were you angry about your past? Hurt? Feeling unworthy of love? Then try some of these as examples or make up your own:

My past does not define me, and my future is bright.

I am worthy of real love.

I can be at peace right now.

I am connected to others more than I know.

Once you find something that really resonates with you, write it down on a card or sticky note, and post it where you will see it daily. Move it to another location when it becomes part of the scenery and loses impact. And to turn this up a notch, say your mantras each morning after you rise, so you can set the intention of keeping the feeling of it in your being.

Remember, you are replacing the darkness you pulled out of yourself with hope and light. And you deserve it.

Therapy: It is proven in research that many people who harm and manipulate others, do not even realize they are doing something wrong. They do not see themselves as an abuser and dismiss this thought, probably thinking, "Those other people need therapy. Not me." Pay attention if this is your thought. If you have not tried journaling, but at least want to talk to someone, find a trusted friend or therapist to talk to.

Whether you can admit that you need this help or not, you will be surprised what you learn about yourself.

Group Sessions: If you are lucky and brave enough to admit that you need help, group sessions are an insightful way to find support. Having other people reflect your thoughts, words and actions back to you because *they use them* too, has a cellular impact. You will realize you are not alone, and you will most likely see parts of yourself that you did not know were there.

Only after you acknowledge them can you heal them.

Case Studies to Inspire Change

In addition to the Case Study Disclaimer mentioned at the beginning of this section, the following studies each focus on a person who has hurt, abused or manipulated others. They are intended as examples to show you that you are not alone in your feelings, and there is hope.

1. The Overwhelmed Mother Who Chose to Break the Cycle

Introduction*:* At age 28, Tanya was raising two young boys on her own. Since most of her waking hours were spent working to pay the bills, the remainder of her hours left her exhausted. She had no work/life balance, and no energy to emotionally support her young children. But Tanya didn't know any better because this was the same way she was raised.

The Struggle: Since Tanya was regularly at her wits' end dealing with stress from work and finances, she often lashed out at her kids when they had an emotional outburst or a need she could not fulfill. After the outbursts, she felt guilty and ashamed. This pattern put her into her own emotional spiral, and she felt like she was drowning in life with no buoy in sight.

The Turning Point: One day, while trying to tidy yet another mess in the living room, she found a picture drawn by her 6-year-old. She froze as she realized it was a picture of her with a dark cloud and a lightning bolt over her head. For the first time, she saw proof that not only were her actions diminishing her spirit, they were setting her kids up to view her as a monster and have no tools to manage their own lives. Though she was exhausted, she knew in her heart that if she could find the strength to change this, their lives could possibly be better. She vowed to get help.

The Outcome: Tanya joined a parenting support group and learned that she wasn't alone. She began practicing small mindfulness techniques that quelled some of her outbursts. And after realizing that the load she carried was just too much, she also enlisted help from an elderly neighbor who enjoyed time with the boys and freed her up for some afterwork motherly duties and even time to journal and stretch. She knew she had made a great difference when she found another drawing months later in the living room. It was a picture of her, but this time her son drew her surrounded with hearts.

Key Takeaway: Breaking generational patterns begins with the courage to be vulnerable and seek help. Parents who are trying to do too much must not only find support to help manage their anger but take some of the pieces off their plate with other community resources and self-care.

2. The Boyfriend Who Saw His Reflection

Introduction: Daniel was a 32-year-old professional. He was handsome and loved that about himself. He did his best to stay fit and buy things that made him look like he was doing well for himself. And he felt he was doing okay. He had to because his dad left their family when he was three years old.

The Struggle: Daniel so badly wanted to settle down and get married, but most of his girlfriends eventually left the relationship and blamed him. How dare they? He really had it going on! Though he didn't realize it, he eventually let the fear of losing his current girl rule his actions. Sometimes he was lucky and could convince them to return after they claimed he emotionally abused them.

The Turning Point: After he took Allison out on their third date, he was hoping she'd stay the night. But as she made some lame excuse of why she couldn't, he got defensive and called her inappropriate names. When she accused him of being mean, he told her it was because she wasn't acknowledging his feelings and needs. She called him a narcissist and started to gather her belongings. A vein popped out of his neck as he yelled and tried to explain what she would be missing when she left because he was such a great catch.

She pulled a mirror from her purse and said, "You think you're so great? Just look at yourself. This is what I see every time you do this to me. Get ahold of yourself. You're no prize. You're just afraid."

He caught a glimpse of himself in that little mirror and was surprised at how ravaged he looked. And when he noticed this, he looked into his own eyes and saw the fear. Allison was right, he was afraid. He begged her to stay, saying he would change, but she stuck her mirror in her purse, said, "Prove it!" and walked out the door.

The Outcome: After doing some reading on the behavior he had so often been called out on, he realized he was using narcissistic tactics, and that's why none of his girlfriends would stay. He was using fear and control to "keep them." Sheepishly, he joined a support group for people who used manipulation techniques and learned that his current actions stemmed from the pain of his past starting when his father left. It took several years, but Daniel is now able to let himself be honest and vulnerable in most of his relationships. He has even been dating a smart woman for almost a year.

Key Takeaway: Sometimes we need to see our reflection to see how others view us. And if we have disruptive patterns in our relationships that we always blame on others, it's time to see how we are contributing to them. Even though it may sting, reaching out for help will always be a critical step if our behaviors perpetually cause others to leave or recoil.

3. The Bully with a Hidden Burden

Introduction: Marcus had a reputation as a bully who disrupted class and taunted his peers. He was slightly larger than most of his fifth-grade classmates and used this to his advantage. He loved the feeling he got when he made somebody cower as he stood over their desk. He felt mighty when he walked down the halls and watched other students hide behind their locker doors. School was where he felt powerful.

The Struggle: At home, however, Marcus faced the same emotional abuse tactics he used on others. Though he didn't fully understand this, the lack of power, love and freedom he felt at home drove his need for finding these feelings in destructive ways.

The Turning Point: One day the school counselor created an optional safe space meet-up during lunch where certain students were invited to attend and share stories. Initially hesitant, Marcus showed up when he saw that one of the girls he had a crush on was attending. Though distracted by the girl, he began to listen to some of the other kids' stories. Many of them were kids he bullied. He felt his tummy do funny things as he watched them cry and sometimes even yell about the way their parents treated them. He knew exactly how they felt, and he decided to share his story as well. It was a shift for everyone when they heard that "Marcus the bully" was also yelled at at home.

The Outcome: Marcus slowly started being nicer to the kids—especially the ones who shared that day. He began to see power in his story, and by the time he was in high school, he became a peer mentor to use his story to encourage empathy among his classmates.

Key Takeaway: Behind disruptive behavior, there is often pain. Stepping in to a safe space, no matter your motive, can be transformative by showing you the hardest parts about yourself in others.

4. The Principal Who Fostered Connection

Introduction: Dr. Martinez was known as a disciplinarian who ran a tight ship as the principal at an alternative school. His credentials had him feeling that he always knew the right answer, and he was quick to enforce proper behavior, correct a problem on scene and reinforce what he thought other people should know as common sense.

The Struggle: After endless conflicts with students resulting in them screaming insults and obscenities at him, Dr. Martinez questioned these outcomes. Why weren't the "rules" working? Why did his approach create distance instead of respect?

The Turning Point: After talking to his wife about it, he realized he was too focused on enforcing rules and therefore missing opportunities to connect to the students. His wife reminded him of many occasions in his own life where he could plainly see that control was not a means for connection. After a few more nights of discussion with her, he decided to join a restorative practice workshop that emphasized listening to students. This worked so well that he continued studying this area of discipline.

The Outcome: Dr. Martinez started integrating his favorite techniques into his daily interactions with the students. One of his simple favorites was greeting each student by name whenever he saw them—an action that seemed arbitrary before. One of his legendary proposals was creating student advisory circles where students could discuss their experiences with or without facilitation from a faculty member. After just a few months of implementing his new strategies, the students had fewer incidents and a stronger sense of belonging. And Dr. Martinez himself felt a much richer sense of purpose in his job.

Key Takeaway: Effective leadership comes from connection, not just correction. A prefix in front of your name does not entitle you to respect. Understanding your role in your position, along with its effect on others and fostering a mutual respect from the start will help you build that in a lasting way.

10

Advocate for Others

Do You Identify?

You see the neighbor boy walking home from school with that look like he's scared to go home again, and it makes your heart ache. You notice how your best friend's boyfriend is always belittling and isolating her, and you want to tell her to leave him. You watch your coworker become withdrawn, and you're so curious but don't know if you should ask about it.

Do you have anyone in your life who, when you see them, your energy shifts to sadness or anger? Not because of something they said or did, but because they seem to be hiding. Are they hiding behind extra layers of clothing? Are they moving so quickly nobody can catch them to ask? Are they smiling in a façade to make you and everyone else believe they are fine?

We already talked about many of the signs that someone is hiding from their hurt. If you see these signs and feel called to help, then I congratulate you.

Validating Your Feelings

Perhaps you are an empath. Perhaps you just love the person you think is hurting. Or maybe you know all about generational cycles and want to help put a stop to one. No matter your role in the situation, let me first thank you for realizing you want to come to somebody's aid. That is a priceless gift if you can do it gracefully—you could perhaps save someone's life.

Steps Forward

Now remember I said this needs to be done gracefully. Here's what I mean.

When we approach survivors and abusers with judgment, we create barriers to healing. We can actually offend or turn someone away from us by harping that something needs to change. If you approach them from a place of compassion and understanding, you have a better chance to open the doors for change. It is important to realize your role isn't to fix them but to create space for healing. You can invite them to improve their life and show them what's possible, but like I said with opening that door, you can't push them through it.

Breaking the cycle of hurt requires education, compassion, and a commitment to move forward. Judgment and shaming reinforce harmful patterns while understanding and empathy create pathways for change.

Here are some ways you can invite and hold that space for someone who wants to live a better life.

Create Safe Spaces for Dialogue: Host workshops or support groups where survivors or abusers can discuss their experiences without fear of judgment. Having people open up around others with the same past experiences and future goals is a powerful way to inspire them to change, find long-term friends and hold themselves accountable for future situations and actions.

Normalize Therapy and Counseling: Advocate for mental health resources in schools, workplaces, and communities. If you are not able to host these yourself, find a program that can. Too many of us have the story that therapy and counseling were not an option either because it was not available, or we were told not to share our business. The more these helpful programs are mainstreamed in communities, the faster we will see that old stigma shift into acceptance and even promotion.

Promote Empathy Through Stories: Share books, films, and personal narratives that illuminate the impact of trauma and the potential for healing. I didn't write this book because I think I'm the only one who has been through it. In fact, I know I'm not. Think about all the stories people have to share. And when they share these stories, they feel empowered! If you can't find personal stories, use your resources of books and films and create a safe space either virtually or in person to host events to share them. It could be as easy as putting one into your social media feed. If one person in need finds it, clicks on it and has a positive experience, you are making a difference.

For Educators: Understanding your own journey creates a compassionate learning environment that encourages students to embrace their stories. Classroom curriculums are always using stories as a way of learning. Why not spend some time on a story your students can relate to in this way? Raising awareness is the first step to have them question the behavior that may be happening in their own home. And so importantly, the more you understand about helping others heal, the bigger impact you can make during your discussions about this. You know the dynamic of your students better than anyone; watch how they shift. Who is being left out? Who is always quiet? You don't have to interrogate them at all, but just getting physically to their level, showing you care and proving you will listen is a great way to offer that invitation for them to walk through that door of healing.

For Mentors and Advocates: Your healing journey sets an example for those you guide, showing them that transformation is possible and worthwhile. No matter your role in someone's life, if you see that they may need help, prove to them that you care. Prove to them that their feelings matter and encourage them to find a safe place to share them—whether it's you or not. Silence is the enemy here. And again, while you don't need to prod the information out of someone, offering a safe ear or an accepting smile is the key to building someone's trust.

Case Studies to Inspire Change

In addition to the Case Study Disclaimer mentioned at the beginning of this section, the following studies each focus on a person who wants to advocate for others. They are intended as examples to show you that you can be a powerful asset when assisting in someone's healing journey.

1. The High School Counselor Who Listened

Introduction: Despite a busy schedule, Ms. Harris was known for making time for her students. She knew that her purpose included more than adhering to meeting times and filling out paperwork. Her "antennae" as some of the other staff called it, were always on to observe the students in her school.

The Struggle: Midway through the year, she noticed that Andre, an ordinarily upbeat senior, had become withdrawn. The glow many of the seniors had when talking about college had worn off him, making him a bit defensive in conversations with his classmates and teachers. Ms. Harris observed this for a full week, making sure his reactions were consistent before approaching him about the subject.

The Turning Point: On Friday, she noticed Andre was standing against the wall by himself before the first bell. She casually stood next to him and smiled kindly at him. After he forced a smile back, she said, "You haven't seemed like yourself lately."

With that notion, he slunk into the wall facing her. He did his best not to cry as he shared that his family was experiencing financial hardship, and he didn't think he would be able to attend the college he had been dreaming of since he was a sophomore. His whole world seemed to fall apart at the thought of it, and it consumed him—especially at school.

The Outcome: Ms. Harris met with Andre twice the following week to help him connect with local support programs. They also figured out which scholarships to apply for and filled the forms out together since she knew many students struggled with this part. They met a couple more times before school ended that year, to follow up on their progress. They had a little dance party in the hall when he told her he got accepted to his pursued school with scholarships that would pay for over half of his tuition. Andre graduated with confidence and feverishly planned for the upcoming year where he would begin attending the college of his choice.

Key Takeaway: Staying observant to the people around you will help you realize when their energy shifts. Once you believe the shift is consistent, and they may need support in altering it for their highest good, find a graceful way to step in and either announce your observation or ask open-ended questions that might get them to open up. When people don't know they have a way out, they can feel stuck in their own despair.

2. The Gas Station Clerk Who Showed Compassion

Introduction: Nadine was the afternoon clerk at a neighborhood convenience store. She saw many kids come in after school for snacks. This was her favorite part of her shift because the kids seemed more upbeat than the adults who would come in during the morning commute stressed out and in a hurry.

The Struggle: Lily, one of the young teens, used to come in for candy or gum sometimes, but she started meandering through the aisles daily without purchasing anything at all. She would also lean on the counter to make small talk with Nadine, which Nadine enjoyed. But Lily seemed to force her smile, and she would often look out the glass doors with a pained look.

Nadine didn't want to say anything right away, but she felt something was off. She waited a few days, and when Lily continued to linger, she figured it would be okay to ask about it.

The Turning Point: One afternoon, while they were the only two people in the store, Nadine asked, "I don't mind if you don't buy anything, but is everything okay?" Lily's eyes got big and started to tear up. She looked around like she didn't think she should say anything, but then the truth suddenly poured out. "It's my mom's new boyfriend. He's so gross and he always gives me these looks when she's not looking, like—like he wants to do things to me. I can't be there when he's there! He works second shift, so I just try to find somewhere else to go until he leaves. I'm sorry. I just don't know where else to go!"

The Outcome: Nadine listened fervently to Lily's woes. And not only did she allow Lily to hang out at the store while her mom's boyfriend was at her house, they devised a plan for how she could tell her mother about what he was doing behind her back. Her mother eventually saw evidence of her boyfriend's behavior and broke up with him. She also reported him to the authorities in hopes of keeping him out of other homes with young ladies.

Since Nadine and Lily had been through so much together, Lily got her first job at the convenience store and eventually got promoted to a managerial position before she graduated high school.

Key Takeaway: Small gestures of kindness can anchor someone during their most challenging times. Having a safe place to take refuge, spending time making a plan and even offering to expand someone's purpose are all great ways to help someone through a tough time.

3. Silent Tension in the Workplace

Introduction: Jordan and Priya, two colleagues, avoided direct communication after a project disagreement. They each blamed each other and secretly waited for the other to apologize. Shortly after this happened, their supervisor noticed he was able to concentrate more because the office had less chatter. He enjoyed this.

The Struggle: The colleagues' miscommunication led to passive-aggressive emails and a total breakdown in collaboration. Neither Jordan nor Priya could concentrate on their work. They instead became fixated on their anger and how to retaliate against the other. Their supervisor, beyond the silence, noticed that tasks, even simple ones, were not getting accomplished by either one of those employees.

He began paying more attention to their behavior and noticed they were both up in arms, red-faced and twitchy in their movements. He remembered the project they worked on a few weeks ago and suddenly remembered hearing about a heated argument from one of their other colleagues. He decided it was time to step in.

The Turning Point: The supervisor facilitated a meeting where they each had time and a safe space to share their perspectives. Though the first words were harsh and aggressive, after hearing each other's side with a mediator, they both began to soften.

The Outcome: With a mediator, they realized that no one was to blame for what went wrong in their project and even realized the mistake was unavoidable. Now it was the management's problem!

Once they were able to laugh about the situation and remove the blame, they started talking like old friends again. They missed their conversations and the camaraderie they shared daily. Their supervisor was relieved to end the animosity, and he watched them rebuild trust and improve team cohesion. But he did have to get used to their chattiness again.

Key Takeaway: Conflict in the workplace often stems from miscommunication. Resolution starts with listening and understanding the other person's perspective. If this can't be done solely with the involved parties, get someone higher up to mediate the situation.

4. The Sibling Who Stepped In

Introduction: Claire, now in college while her two younger sisters were still in high school, felt responsible for their emotional well-being after their parents' separation. She felt like she could see it from a higher perspective since her life wasn't upturned as much as theirs was when their father moved out of the house. Each sister would call Claire at least twice a week for consolation.

The Struggle: Claire bottled up her own emotions about the divorce and instead focused on her sisters. She never took the time to grieve for herself since she was always trying to quell their emotions. As the heavy feelings that come with unprocessed grief would bubble up, she started distracting herself by studying harder and taking on extra programs.

The Turning Point: Her college mentor noticed this shift in her emotional well-being. Claire's "can-do" attitude now felt forced and excessive while the light in her eyes became dim. After several attempts and zero breakthroughs in finding out what was going on with Claire, the mentor took a different approach. "If you feel the need to keep yourself so busy, why don't you journal at the end of each day?"

The Outcome: Claire found a journal that felt great in her hands, and she started journaling about the day's events and accomplishments. After a few days, though, her emotions started coming through. Instead of scribing the standard page about the day's events, she would fill page after page about how angry she was at her mom and how sad she was for her father. The pages became stained with tears as her heart poured out. She couldn't believe the change that took place and the lightness she felt after purging so much grief. She made sure to thank her mentor for the suggestion, and by that time, she was even ready to talk to her about what her family was going through. She also became a better beacon for her siblings and started to be able to calm them instead of igniting them further.

Key Takeaway: Even the strongest, oldest and most honored people in our lives need a space to feel vulnerable and express what's bottled up. You can do someone a huge favor by creating a safe space for someone to heal—even if it's in their journal.

Books and Resources

Childhood Disrupted by Donna Jackson Nakazawa

Helping Abused and Traumatized Children by Eliana Gil

The Deepest Well by Dr. Nadine Burke Harris

Books for Educators

The Boy Who Was Raised as a Dog by Dr. Bruce Perry

Fostering Resilient Learners by Kristin Souers & Pete Hall

Helping Traumatized Children Learn by Massachusetts Advocates for Children

The Invisible Classroom by Kirke Olson

11

Victims and Survivors

Do You Identify?

If you are a victim or a survivor, you might feel heavy. You are exhausted. You are drowning in your life and quite possibly feel that every possible path to safety will get you into more trouble. When you see your reflection, you may not even recognize who you have become.

Your body might physically ache. Your head spins whenever "they" come around, and you just do not know what will trigger them next.

Whether you are still in your traumatic situation or are able to look back at it, one thing you can be thankful for is that you are still alive. Whether that seems like a blessing or a curse right now, you still have time to climb out of the darkness and a chance to be of service to others using your experience. You have time to heal, and hopefully this book will give you the tools, time and space to do that.

It's quite likely that you have a lot of negative self-talk going on as I did when I first tried to get on with a regular life while carrying bags full of nagging emotions. This may seem like an unfathomable task to tackle, but you can do it.

Validating Your Feelings

Please know that all those heavy, dark, defeating feelings you have are normal for an individual in your situation. Those feelings are telling you something is not right. Without them, you may not know something is wrong, and you wouldn't try to break free. Free from the abuse you may still be in or free from the pain that dims your light.

Feeling these negative emotions is a good driving force for change. You might feel broken. You might feel betrayed. You might feel like everything is too much, but there is something inside of you that is stronger than what anyone else can do or say to you. I hope I proved that with my own story.

The point of all this is that it's important for you to admit what you are feeling. The more you try to hide your feelings, the more it comes out in symptomatic ways like isolation, fake smiles and laughing at something that is simply not funny. Surrendering to how you feel without judging yourself is the first step toward igniting change.

Steps Forward

You've been through some trauma and heartache, and you now have scars. But your scars are badges of courage, and your story can become a light for others still searching for their own way.

Many of the inspirational and influential people you see out there today have scars. Some of them will tell you their story, but not all of them will. It is my belief that the more influential people share their scar's stories, the more we will feel we have permission to reveal our own, to know we are not alone and to believe we can be something more.

People don't decide to change or try hard when they've had an easy life. Change is not necessary in those rare cases, so please understand that sometimes it is necessary for us to feel the pain and the darkness. Once we learn the blessings from the darkness, we can start our journey of healing and become a catalyst to spark change in others.

If you are still in an abusive situation, get help. You may not want to do this, but sometimes you must get the authorities involved. They will hold that other person accountable and possibly make an arrangement where they are not allowed to contact or go near you. If you need this kind of protection, please do what you need to do to save your life.

Maybe your situation is not that dire. Maybe you can just leave and hope you never see your abuser again. When choosing this route, make sure you have someone else looking out for you and checking in on you. Get some accountability on your whereabouts. Not only will this keep you physically safer, it will give you more peace of mind and keep your stress level down, so you can make better decisions as you move forward.

Once you are out of your situation, you are going to have some healing to do. Here are some ways to get yourself started:

Read: Believe it or not, there are thousands and thousands of people who are feeling the same as you right now. And there is a big movement for survivors of trauma to write a book to tell their own story. These stories are powerful. They are inspiring. And they are true. Search for a couple titles that seem like they will resonate with you either online, in the library or at a bookstore.

Videos and other online content can serve you as well. I don't recommend spending all your time on the internet, as a book is healthier for your mind, but whatever helps you take that first step toward your own healing is the catalyst you need and deserve.

Journal: If you're not ready to express your innermost pain to somebody else, at least express it to yourself. You don't need to buy a snazzy notepad, but if it helps you want to write in it, go ahead and motivate yourself with a journal that speaks to you.

Get your stories out of your mind and onto paper. It doesn't even matter if you never read them again; the physical and mental act of writing your thoughts and purging your emotions opens a powerful door toward healing. Even if it's just a couple sentences a day. Those sentences might turn into pages and, once you are healed and have forgiven, you just might write one of those helpful books you ran to in your moment of need.

Therapy: We've already talked about the fact that this can have a negative connotation, but do you know what? It's just not true. A brain is a brain. A neuron is a neuron. Each human brain on a functioning adult has a fundamental system it follows to function, learn and rewire itself. Therapists are trained in this. They can tell you the patterns you might be cycling in before you even realize it.

They know this stuff.

And they can help you unlearn the harmful patterns and thoughts you've adapted while you were in your traumatic situation(s). They can show you how to reframe your thinking into empowering thoughts and patterns. And if they can't, find a different person to talk to. You deserve the best treatment to let your light shine. The light you came to this earth with. It's inside you waiting for the dust to clear.

Trusted Friend: If you're not ready for therapy, find a trusted friend. You will need a safe space to be able to tell your stories in, and to have somebody validate your feelings is priceless. Once you get your old stories out, you might cry, swear, blame and scream. But what else happens when you let out that old stuff?

You make room for the new. Just like in a closet.

Once you release the pain you kept inside, you no longer need to harbor it. It's free, and you're free to fill it with love, compassion and visions of the best version of yourself. Use that trusted friend to bounce ideas off. Talk to them about your goals. A truly good friend will let you rant, scream, dream and cry without judgement. They will let you be you, and they can remind you how much they love you and that you deserve a better life. They may even walk beside you on your journey of healing.

Support Groups: If you need to immerse yourself in people who have been there and who understand, join a support group. These can be facilitated by a professional or simply be a gathering of wounded individuals who are working on their scars.

The value of validation when you hear someone tell the story of what they went through and you can think or say, "Yes! They did that to me too! I know how you feel!" is priceless for you and for them. The camaraderie that is built in these settings can be infinite.

Who knows who you might meet? The perspectives you might gain can truly be life changing on their own. Find your people. Find new friends. Put yourself in a safe place with others who have shared your pain in their own lives, so you can rise together.

Start or Reignite Interests and Hobbies: Depending on when your abuse started, you might have lived a seemingly normal life before. You may have had hobbies, jobs, education, dreams, etc. Whether you had pastimes you'd like to recreate or new ideas to start, the time is now.

I'm not telling you to do these things instead of seeking a friend, a group session or a therapist. I'm telling you to do this also. Don't just use a new hobby or exercise or more education to distract yourself from facing your pain like I did at first. That doesn't solve the problem. It keeps it in the dark.

Start your healing journey from within *and* find positive, motivating, dream-building activities to get yourself into. It will help shape who you want to be. It will keep you focused on the present and future instead of the past. You don't want to linger in the past, so start planning your life in a way that retrains your brain to remind you that you are capable, worthy and on your way to a new life.

Mantras and Meditation: Once you've done the work to recognize you are a worthy human being, you need to remind yourself of that often. I had several mantras I repeated to myself so I could quickly elevate my thoughts when I got into a funk.

As you go through therapy, talk to a friend, journal, attend a support group, or read a good book, pay attention to the short phrases that jump out at you. You will know them the moment you read or hear them. They will sting in a good way. Write them down as soon as you can and repeat them whenever necessary.

Your mantras can be quick, powerful tools to help you return your frame of mind back to your deserving self.

Layers of trauma help to pile on layers of anxiety. You can observe this by noticing how quickly or easily your patience wanes and your annoyance builds. When you feel this shift into a more panicked state, take a deep breath. It may sound cliché, but that's because it works. Your breath is what connects your body to the physical atmosphere by taking in oxygen. It feels comfortably connecting and refreshing to take a breath. It calms your brain and encourages it to think from the more evolved areas instead of the primal ones.

Breathing steadily with focus and intention will help to calm your nerves, bring you back to a homeostasis and allow you to make better decisions as you carry on throughout your day.

If you want to take this up a notch, try meditation. It can help you get into a calm state for longer and even more readily return to it when needed. You will most likely be able to find a great meditation easily online or from any of the other tools listed above.

Case Studies to Inspire Change

In addition to the Case Study Disclaimer mentioned at the beginning of this section, the following studies each focus on a person who either resides in a fearful situation or has previously escaped. They are intended as examples to show you that you are not alone in your struggles, and there is hope.

1. The Student Who Found Safety at School

Introduction: Jasmine was a quiet seventh grader who always tried to sit in the back of the classroom or behind a tall kid. She was slow to catch on to new material, and her new teacher wondered if she needed a 504.

Her hair wasn't always brushed like the other girls, and they teased her for sleeping in her clothes, which she did. She could often be found dozing off in the mornings and after lunch.

The Struggle: Jasmine didn't get much sleep at home. She brushed her hair and put on her clothes before bed because she knew she would be awake most of the night while her parents fought. Whether she chose to listen or cover her face with her pillow, she was terrified when this happened. Not only did she hear them yelling, she heard dishes break, doors slam and fists pound.

She hated being at home. She couldn't wait to roll out of bed, grab her backpack and walk to school. Ever since the fighting started, school was her refuge, but she was too afraid to tell anyone, and too tired to come up with a solution.

The Turning Point: One day Jasmine remained asleep at her desk while the class dismissed for gym. Her homeroom teacher, Ms. Rivera, put her hand on her shoulder and quietly asked, "Jasmine, is this the only place you get to sleep?"

Tears welled up as Jasmine opened her eyes and realized she was the only student left in the room. Her parents were ruining her life, and now it was obvious. "I'm sorry, Ms. Rivera. I'm so sorry. I don't sleep at home. My parents are too loud when they scream at each other like every night."

Ms. Rivera realized her suspicions were right, and recommended Jasmine speak with the guidance counselor.

The Outcome: The school counselor developed a support plan for Jasmine. It included reaching out to other students who had a place for her to sleep a couple nights a week. Once her parents caught on to Jasmine's absence, they realized they were not only hurting themselves, they were hurting their daughter. They decided to go to marriage counseling to have a mediator and let their daughter get some sleep. In her own bed.

Jasmine was surprised and relieved at how she could create change in others by making a change on her own. This empowered her as she grew older, and she went on to inspire other teens to take control of their own lives.

Key Takeaway: The students who sleep in class aren't always bored or defiant. They could be seeking refuge. A simple question can open the door to healing and empower them into lasting change throughout the facets of their life.

2. The Burned-Out Teacher

Introduction: Mr. Ellis was a passionate fourth grade teacher. Most of the third graders dreamed of being in his class the following year as he was known for his creative lessons and engaging personality. However, in his 11th year of teaching, his energy waned. Student engagement dropped in his class as he seemed to lose interest. His participation in meetings was either withdrawn or volatile. Both the students and the staff wondered what was going on, but nobody asked right away, hoping he would feel better soon.

The Struggle: Mr. Ellis was navigating a difficult divorce. His wife found another man, and he felt like a failure. How could the most desired teacher at school not be desirable to his wife at home?

This thought not only drained him, but it started making him doubt his true abilities as a teacher. He became self-conscious about his every move and stuffed his authenticity in a dark corner of his body.

The Turning Point: One afternoon as his students were filing out for dismissal, Peyton, one of his smartest students, turned and said, "Mr. Ellis, I miss your smile. Where did it go?"

This sincere question hit him like a brick wall, but the place it came from made the corner of his mouth grin. "I guess I better work on getting it back," he said.

"Yeah!" Peyton cheered. She hugged Mr. Ellis and ran out the door.

Mr. Ellis took a moment to gather himself. Was he really that obvious? Had he let it go that far? He decided he better get some help.

The Outcome: Mr. Ellis sought support through a one-on-one therapist and a group meeting for people whose spouses had done something similar to what his wife did. He began setting boundaries, so he could maintain his time and energy. He also found his stash of keepsakes from students and read them all one by one. This helped remind him that he really was that big-hearted, wonderful teacher, and not even his wife could take that away from him—*or* the students.

Once he came out on top of this, he became an advocate for mental health among educators, reminding them that they are wonderful too.

Key Takeaway: Sometimes, the strongest leaders need someone to remind them that asking for help is okay. And sometimes the most loved individuals need to be reminded of their worth.

3. **The Boyfriend Who Thought Love Should Hurt**

Introduction: Angelina and Hakeem had been dating for three months. Hakeem knew that Angelina had to be "the one" because shortly after they met, she said she knew they were "Twin Flames" and were meant to be. They had already moved in together! He felt a whirlwind of bliss as he felt so lucky to find a beautiful woman who adored him… most of the time.

The Struggle: The times she didn't adore him were frightening and confusing. He never understood what he did wrong until she was up in his face with accusations, interrogations and insults. Each time he questioned her, she got so dramatic he felt like the life got sucked out of him. Sometimes he didn't even feel safe, but he didn't think she would ever hurt him physically.

During the moments she did adore him, he swooned so hard he wanted to propose. "Maybe true love just comes with difficult times and misunderstandings," he thought.

The Turning Point: One day, as Hakeem rode the subway home from work, he saw a similar situation happen right before his eyes. He watched how the man treated the woman, and it was just like how Angelina treated him! He couldn't believe the similarities. It was almost like they used the same script!

He turned to the old lady next to him and asked, "Do you see what is happening there?" The lady glanced up from her book and said, "Classic narcissist if you ask me. She's got to get out of there while she can. I hope they don't have kids." And she went back to reading.

Hakeem didn't go straight home (even though he knew he'd be punished), but he stopped at a guy friend's house to talk about it and do some research. What he found astonished him. He had to get out too!

The Outcome: Hakeem enlisted help from a couple friends who were savvy to the situation and the type of abuse and manipulation someone like Angelina was capable of. They devised a plan to help him move his things out when she was at work. He found a temporary place to live, so he could get out safely and quickly. The only thing he left was a note that read: "I was wrong."

He realized that even though he left, he still had a lot of fear. He ultimately moved to a suburb on the other side of the city and got therapy to help him cope with the new thought patterns she had driven into his brain.

Key Takeaways: Love should never cause harm or fear. Feeling unsafe should prompt you to find some support to help you get out of your situation safely.

4. The "Different" Kid Who Got Teased

Introduction: Jayce was a sweet sixth grader. He had a small frame, and his auditory system hadn't fully developed externally or internally which left the bottom of his earlobes adhered to his head and gave him a slight speech impediment. Many of the kids in his class adored him because he was such a caring friend, but one kid, Walter, took every opportunity he could to pick on Jayce.

The Struggle: Walter was mean, but he was also keen. Any chance he could catch Jayce without anyone else around, he would whisper horrible things to him. "Hey, retard. *Hear* any good jokes lately? I bet you didn't!" Walter would laugh and walk away before anyone could see that Jayce had frozen, holding back tears. Again.

This went on for weeks, but Jayce didn't think he could tell anyone. He was so afraid of the way Walter made him feel, he just clammed up and went inside his shell.

The Turning Point: Their homeroom teacher, Ms. Jackson noticed Jayce becoming increasingly closed off and paranoid. When she asked him about it, he said nothing was wrong, but she could read behind his eyes.

While the students went to their lockers one afternoon, Ms. Jackson stood behind her door and listened as best she could.

"Hey dummy. Want to read me a story later, so I can laugh at how stupid you sound?"

But before Walter could run off, Ms. Jackson appeared like a phantom out of the shadows—with no mercy.

"Excuse me, Walter," she leered, "Would you like to read me a story in detention?"

The Outcome: Walter was reprimanded fully for his behavior toward another student. Plus, Ms. Jackson told each student individually to keep a special eye out for Walter and Jayce and report any negative interactions they observed. All the students agreed and stood up for their friend without belittling Walter. They knew Walter had his own faults, but protecting the little guy seemed more important than demeaning the big one.

Noticing this dynamic shift, Walter stopped harassing Jayce and even grew to like him. He was a good friend after all.

Key Takeaways: It can be difficult for a person who feels like they might be "less than" to stand up for themselves. It's helpful to watch out for these people, no matter how old or young they are. Make sure they are getting the support and protection they need without demeaning the person who might be ridiculing them.

Books and Resources

The Choice: Embrace the Possible by Dr. Edith Eger

Second Firsts: Live, Laugh, and Love Again by Christina Rasmussen

12

Encouragement

You are well on your way to a meaningful future. But remember, healing and forgiveness are not destinations—they are journeys that lead to a life filled with joy, fulfillment, and growth. Life beyond the hurt is not about forgetting the past—it's about reclaiming your story and transforming your pain into strength.

I would like to say that again: You can transform your pain into strength!

Life beyond the hurt is where your scars become your badges of courage, and your story becomes your light for others still searching for their way. When you look at it and live in it through this perspective, you can become empowered!

Here is a transformational chant for your scars.

S.C.A.R.S. Chant

Strength is in my story—I will not hide.
Courage guides me—I walk with pride.
Accepting my past, I choose to heal.
Rebuilding my future, my power is real.
Shining beyond the scars—I am whole, I am free!

Imagine waking up one day no longer feeling the weight of resentment or regret. The air feels lighter, the world looks brighter, and your reflection carries a quiet, blossoming confidence.

This is the power of healing.

It is powerful. It is liberating. And it is priceless.

But like you saw with my journey, it is not easy, nor is it quick.

I have done my best to share my stories, daily mantras, journal prompts, tools and resources to keep you on your path. If you falter, choose a different tool and start again. Your journey will continue, and your smile is worth it.

Like I said in the previous section, I can now use my smile as a beam of hope to others. Not just a place to hide.

Here is an inspirational chant to encourage your smile.

S.M.I.L.E. Chant

See my light—it cannot be dimmed.
My heart beats strong, I rise again.
I am worthy, I stand in grace.
Love and truth shine on my face.
Every smile proves my strength—I am healed, I am here!

When I coach others, speak to a large group, or mentor through educator enhancement programs, I help everyday heroes sitting among victims of trauma to notice the signs in others. This knowledge can make the difference in a student, coworker, family member, or friend who you think might be struggling with a difficult situation.

To all my educators and advocates out there, thank you. For you (and me), I've designed the R.I.S.E. acronym, and I share it across my platforms.

Recognize the signs of hidden struggles

Invite connection and conversation with empathy

Support without judgment or assumption

Empower the person to take steps toward healing and growth

Take what you will from this book. I hope you have found more than you need to propel you on your journey. You are not your past, and you are not your pain. You are the person who chooses to rise above it, who turns scars into strength, and who inspires others to do the same. Keep striving for a better life for yourself and others. Your gifts are important; use the tools you've learned here to uncover them and wow the world.

Your gifts matter.

And your experiences matter. Your hardest moments are the catalyst for connecting to someone who may be in your situation now. Please remember that you are worthy of a meaningful life because that in itself will inspire others.

And when you smile, may your smile be the result of the joy you embody.

Appendix and Journal Prompts

Reflection & Journal Prompts for Survivors

Use these prompts to guide self-discovery, healing, and resilience

Recognizing Your Strength

- What is one challenge from your past that you have already overcome?
- How did you find the strength to get through it?

Healing the Inner Child

- If you could speak to your younger self, what words of encouragement would you offer?
- What did you need to hear as a child that you never received? Write it now.
- What affectionate nicknames have shaped your identity within your family?
- How do these names reflect your relationships and personal growth?
- Write a letter embracing these endearing terms to explore their impact on your journey.

The Power of Boundaries

- What are some ways you can protect your peace and emotional well-being?
- How do you respond when someone crosses your boundaries?

Reclaiming Your Voice

- What is one thing you have been afraid to say out loud?
- What is holding you back from expressing it?

Gratitude & Moving Forward

- Name three things you are grateful for today.
- What is one small step you can take to prioritize your healing?

Books For Personal Growth & Understanding Trauma

Daring Greatly—Brené Brown

Atomic Habits—James Clear

The Gifts of Imperfection—Brené Brown

The Grieving Brain—Mary Frances O'Connor

Support Hotlines & Online Resources

For survivors, educators, and advocates

National Domestic Violence Hotline (U.S.)

1-800-799-SAFE (7233) Text "START" to 88788 thehotline.org

National Child Abuse Hotline (Childhelp—U.S.)

1-800-4-A-CHILD (1-800-422-4453) childhelp.org/hotline

RAINN (Rape, Abuse & Incest National Network—U.S.) 1-800-656-HOPE (4673) rainn.org

Love Is Respect (For Teens & Young Adults Experiencing Dating Abuse)

1-866-331-9474 Text "LOVEIS" to 22522 loveisrespect.org

National Alliance on Mental Illness (NAMI—U.S.)

1-800-950-NAMI (6264) Text "HELPLINE" to 62640 nami .org

International Support Hotlines:

UK Domestic Abuse Helpline—0808 2000 247 nationalda helpline.org.uk

Canada Assaulted Women's Helpline—1-866-863-0511 awhl .org

Australia 1800RESPECT (DV & Trauma Support)—1800 737 732 1800respect.org.au

Resources for Educators Working with At-Risk Children & Domestic Violence Victims

Educators play a critical role in identifying and supporting at-risk students. The following books, training programs, and online resources help teachers, school counselors, and administrators recognize trauma and create a safe, supportive environment for children facing domestic violence or abuse.

Child Trauma Academy—childtrauma.org

Sesame Street in Communities—Trauma Resources for Kids —sesamestreetincommunities.org

National Child Traumatic Stress Network (NCTSN)—Educator Toolkit—nctsn.org

Safe & Sound Schools (School Safety & Trauma Support)—safeandsoundschools.org

Mental Health First Aid (Training for Schools & Youth Workers)—mentalhealthfirstaid.org

Final Notes

This appendix serves as a resource guide for survivors, educators, and advocates who want to recognize, understand, and support those impacted by trauma and domestic violence. If you or someone you know is struggling, please reach out! Help is available! You are not alone.

Works Cited

Hughes, K., Bellis, M. A., Hardcastle, K. A., Sethi, D., Butchart, A., Mikton, C., Jones, L., & Dunne, M. P. (2017). *The effect of multiple adverse childhood experiences on health: a systematic review and meta-analysis.* The Lancet Public Health, 2(8), e356–e366. This comprehensive study examines the cumulative impact of multiple adverse childhood experiences (ACEs) on health outcomes, highlighting the strong association between ACEs and various mental health issues, including depression, anxiety, and substance abuse. The findings underscore the profound long-term effects of childhood trauma on mental health and relationships.

Neff, K. (2011). *Self-Compassion: The Proven Power of Being Kind to Yourself.* New York, NY: HarperCollins.

National Institute of Mental Health. (2023). *Self-Esteem and Mental Health.* Retrieved from https://www.nimh.nih.gov

American Psychological Association. (2023). *Understanding Self-Esteem.* Retrieved from https://www.apa.org

Jay, T., & Jay, T. (2013). *A Child's Garden of Curses: A Gender, Historical, and Age-Related Evaluation of the Taboo Lexicon.* The American Journal of Psychology, 126(4), 459–475.

Excellence vs. Perfection. (n.d.). Anonymous. Retrieved from https://nasad.arts-accredit.org/wp-content/uploads/sites/3/2021/04/excellence.perfection. pdf

Rushnell, S. (2002). *When God Winks: How the Power of Coincidence Guides Your Life.* Atria Books.

Gould, W. R. (2024, December 27). *9 subtle ways you seem insecure without realizing it.* Verywell Mind.

This article explores various behaviors that may indicate underlying insecurities, such as over-apologizing, difficulty accepting compliments, and social withdrawal. It provides insights into how these subtle signs can impact personal and professional relationships and offers strategies to address them.

Carter-Scott, C. (1989). *Negaholics: How to Overcome Negativity and Turn Your Life Around.* Ballantine Books.

Oxford Learner's Dictionaries. (n.d.). *One-upmanship.* In Oxford Advanced American Dictionary. Retrieved from https://www.oxfordlearnersdictionaries.com/definition/english/one-Upmanship

Acknowledgments

No journey is ever walked alone, and this book is no exception. *Behind Every Smile: How to Spot and Support Victims of Trauma* results from years of reflection, healing, and the unwavering support of many incredible people.

To Luvvie Ajayi Jones and The Book Academy, where my journey as an author truly began. As a founding member, I found guidance and a community that shaped this book's foundation. Luvvie and her team have been my God Wink, a divine confirmation that I was walking in my purpose. Thank you for your wisdom and encouragement and for showing me what is possible when we dare to write our truth.

To Amanda Wais and my editorial team, I am deeply grateful. Your editorial expertise helped refine and shape my story while keeping my voice intact. Thank you for your skillful editing, insight and unwavering support in bringing my drafts to their fullest potential. This book would not be what it is without your guidance in molding my words to their most impactful form.

To my mentors and coaches, whose wisdom and encouragement helped me fully understand my purpose. Your guidance in leadership, personal growth, and business development gave me the confidence to bring this book to life.

To my chosen family and dearest friends, the ones who cheered me on (you know who you are), lifted me up, and reminded me that I was never alone in this journey—your unwavering support means more than words can express.

To every survivor, advocate, and reader who finds themselves in these pages—thank you. Your courage, your stories, and your voices matter. May this book bring you the healing, hope, and empowerment you deserve.

And above all, **to God**, the ultimate author of my story. Every God Wink, every whisper of encouragement, and every moment of grace has led me here. Thank You for guiding me through the valleys and helping me rise.

With deep gratitude,

Natatia Vanellison

About the Author

Founder and CEO, NaTaTiaCoaching, LLC™ | Award-Winning Educator | Distinguished Toastmaster (DTM) | Certified Virtual Presenter (CVP) | Transformational Speaker | Author

Natatia Vanellison is an award-winning educator, leadership mentor, and transformational career coach with over thirty-one years of experience. The Founder and CEO of NaTaTiaCoaching, LLC™, she is dedicated to empowering women over forty who feel unseen, unheard and undervalued in their careers.

Through her signature coaching programs—the R.I.S.E. Leadership Accelerator™ and the Synergy Empowerment Leadership Accelerator™—she equips leaders with the confidence, strategies and resilience to rise to their full potential.

As a Distinguished Toastmaster (DTM) and Certified Virtual Presenter (CVP), she has a deep passion for public speaking, leadership development and empowering women to use their voices with confidence. She has chartered three Toastmasters clubs, including one designed to prepare speakers and empower women leaders through storytelling, executive presence, and strategic communication.

Throughout her extensive career in education, she worked in leadership development, mentoring both high school students and adults to cultivate confidence, resilience and professional impact.

Her dedication to education and leadership has earned prestigious awards, further solidifying her role as a recognized expert in mentoring, coaching and professional development.

She is a founding member of The Book Academy®, established by four-time New York Times bestselling author and TEDx speaker Luvvie Ajayi Jones. Having successfully graduated from all three of Luvvie's cohort programs, she is now part of the Alumni Accelerator Program, an exclusive initiative for advanced authors.

Beyond her professional endeavors, she is deeply grateful for the unwavering support of her husband, whom she lovingly describes as "the most supportive husband on the planet." His encouragement has been an anchor throughout her tumultuous journey, reinforcing her mission to empower others to be seen, heard, and valued.

www.ingramcontent.com/pod-product-compliance
Ingram Content Group UK Ltd.
Pitfield, Milton Keynes, MK11 3LW, UK
UKHW042016190726
13854UKWH00005B/2303